D1565445

Vern L. Bengtson

The Social
Psychology
of Aging

THE BOBBS-MERRILL STUDIES IN SOCIOLOGY

The Social Psychology of Aging

Vern L. Bengtson

THE BOBBS-MERRILL COMPANY, INC.
INDIANAPOLIS • NEW YORK

Third Printing

Library of Congress Cataloging in Publication Data

Bengtson, Vern L.
The social psychology of aging.

(The Bobbs-Merrill studies in sociology)
Bibliography: p.
1. Aged—United States. 2. Aging. I. Title.
[DNLM: 1. Aging. 2. Social behavior—In old age.
WT 150 B466s 1973]
HQ1064.U5B37   301.43'5'0973   73'-4918
ISBN O-672-61339-5 (pbk.)

The Social Psychology of Aging

1: Time, Change, and Everyday Behavior: Issues in the Sociology of Age
   A. Age Differences in Everyday Behavior
   B. Dimensions of Change Over Time: Developmental and Historical
      1. Developmental Time and Developmental Events: The Maturational Effect
      2. Historical Time and Historical Events: The Cohort Effect
   C. Dimensions of Social Structure: Interpersonal and Institutional Contexts
      1. Elements of Social Organization
      2. Age and the Interpersonal Context
      3. Age and the Institutional Context

2: Aging and the Social System
   A. Social Age and Developmental Time
   B. Socialization and the Social System
      1. Social Age and Age Grading
      2. Age Norms
      3. Norms in Old Age
      4. Normlessness: Negative and Positive Consequences
      5. Age Roles, Stereotypes, and Role Loss in Old Age
      6. Old Age and Reference Groups
      7. The Social System and Adult Socialization

3: Aging and the Personal System
   A. Personality Traits or Motives and Aging
      1. Covert vs. Overt Personality Processes
      2. Personality Typologies
   B. Aging and Self-Concept
   C. Life Style and Aging
   D. Patterns of Aging

4: Theories of Aging: Scientific and Applied
   A. The Current State of Theory in Social Gerontology
   B. Activity Theory of Aging
   C. Disengagement Theory
   D. The Social Reconstruction Model
      1. Emergent Perspectives in Theory Building
      2. The "Social Reconstruction Syndrome"

5: Summary
References and Suggested Readings

This monograph has benefited much from the careful reading and comments of several colleagues: Judith Huff, Monica Morris, Pauline Ragan, Patricia Kasschau, LaMar Empey, Barbara Buckwalter, Dean Black, Fred Richardson, Janis Pulliam; and especially from the suggestions of Robert Atchley and Nina Nahemow. The clerical assistance of Ingrid McClendon was invaluable.

I want to acknowledge the support of the National Institutes of Mental Health whose grant (#MH-18158, "Generational Differences: Correlates and Consequences") enabled the collection of data and development of concepts on which much of this volume is based.

An earlier draft of this paper was prepared for the summer institutes program of the Andrus Gerontology Center, University of Southern California, under the direction of James Birren and Ruth Weg.

1 Time, Change, and Everyday Behavior: Issues in the Sociology of Age

The subject of this essay is continuity and change in social behavior with the passage of time. The central theme is that behavior at each stage of an individual's life should be viewed as the product of dynamic interaction between the social system and the personal system, as each system reflects both stability and change over time. On the one hand, there is change as the individual negotiates the many events that occur as he or she grows up and grows old—events which are social, psychological, biological, and historical in nature. On the other hand, there is continuity: behavior is the product of the individual's personal history of adaptation to the varying social contexts and biopsychological issues that occur with the passage of time.

A social psychology of aging, therefore, examines phenomena of change and continuity over time in both the social system and personal system of individuals as they progress through the normal course of the life-cycle. In the sections to follow we will first analyze the developing individual from the perspective of the ever-changing social context in which he plays out his roles and relationships through the course of his life. Then we will look at the personal system—the individual's long-term adaptations to those changes in terms of personality dispositions and life style. We will conclude with a discussion of theories of aging—attempts to integrate the many facts concerning continuity and change in the social and personal systems of people as they age.

AGE DIFFERENCES IN EVERYDAY BEHAVIOR

To begin our analysis of these complex issues, let us look briefly at the life history, attitudes, and behaviors of three individuals who are at different points in the human life-cycle. The three are members of the same family: a grandfather, his middle-aged son, and a young adult grandson.

Johann Johnson, age 73:
   Retired against his will from a factory job eight years ago, he spends much of his time gardening, listening to religious radio programs, and talking with friends at the union local which has a senior citizens cen-

5

ter. His income is less than $400 per month but he considers himself well off compared to some of his acquaintances who are living on Social Security alone. He gets around well despite severe loss of movement from a broken hip. Born in Sweden, he describes his "most important events in life" as follows: came to America as a five-year-old; lost a good farm during the Depression because of speculation; started making good money in a factory during World War II; lost wife from cancer in 1970. He voted for Harding, Landon, Dewey, and Goldwater. His friends describe him as hard-working, vigorous, honest, knowledgeable, blunt, and opinionated, but say he has "mellowed" in the last five years. He says he doesn't have any goals any more—"only young people have goals"—and that his only concern is to "keep active—I want to wear out, not rust out."

He answers questions in our research questionnaire as follows:
Best thing that could happen to you: "To see our nation return to God."
Worst thing that could happen to you: "To lose my health, which is excellent."
Self-rated liberal to conservative: "Very conservative."
Church attendance: "Every week, when I can get a ride."
Rating on general happiness scale: "Very happy."

Archie Johnson, age 48:
Spends 45 hours per week as an engineer for an aerospace contractor. His salary is good for his position ($22,000) but he works harder than he did a decade ago because in 1970 he was laid off and drew unemployment compensation (a "dole" as he puts it) for 18 months before finding a new job. "I have to put more time in to compete with the younger guys," he says. He describes the most important events in his life thus: ran away from home to join the Navy in 1942, fathered two children, got a college degree on the G.I. bill while supporting his family, got a house in the suburbs. His friends describe him as serious, honest, tense, overly responsible, but warm and generous. Although he voted for Truman, Kennedy, Johnson, and Humphrey, he displayed a Nixon-Agnew bumper sticker for months before and after the 1972 campaign "because the Democratic party has been taken over by radicals and doesn't care about the majority American any more." He has a carefully ordered list of goals for the next year—economic, social, and self-development—which he and his wife go over every three months. This helps him plan, he says—"I have to start thinking about retirement."

His questionnaire shows the following answers:
Best thing that could happen to you: "To see my children grow and make the world a better place."
Worst thing that could happen to you: "To lose my job."
Self-rated liberal to conservative: "Slightly conservative."
Church attendance: "About once a month."

Rating on happiness scale: "Pretty happy."
Rating on marital happiness scale: "Not too happy."

Kirk Johnson, age 23:

Says he spends most of his time during the week "studying with time out for meditating and turning on." He is finishing his degree in sociology at a local state college. He is slightly older than most of his classmates because he dropped out for a year to hitchhike around Canada when it appeared that his draft number had a high probability of being called. He responds to the question about health with one brief word: "great." His friends describe him as intense, genuine, concerned, giving, and friendly. He lives with Joan, a sophomore nursing student, and enjoys seeing his parents wince when he asserts that he and his "old woman" have no intention of getting married—ever. He's proud of the fact that they together live on less than $300 per month but says his mother feels humiliated about his castoff clothing. He was very active in the radical movement on campus when he was a sophomore, but today says he's completely turned off by politics. He at first does not want to talk about his life goals—"Hanging loose and acting on feelings is very important to me"—but then talks animatedly about his desire to become a social worker, to have a career helping people, to form an urban commune which will really last, and to work for world peace.

Answers to questionnaire:

Best thing that could happen to you in life: "To have the world free from war and everyone to be my brother."
Worst thing: "To have someone tell me I can't do my own thing."
Self-rated liberal to conservative: He wrote in "radical."
Church attendance: "Never."
Rating on happiness scale: "Not too happy."

Here are three generations of the same family, three ages of man. We see distinct differences in the behaviors reported between the youth, the middle aged, and the elderly. Data from the Study of Generations and Mental Health at the University of Southern California suggest such differences between generations are not unusual—even though respondents are related and therefore similar in many respects. In this study, involving over 2,100 family members, the grandparents attach more importance to religious participation than the youth. They rate themselves as much more conservative, politically. The middle aged rank the value of "achievement" higher than do the other two generations. And, interestingly enough, the scores on the "happiness" scale are highest for the grandparents, slightly lower for the middle aged, and lowest for the youth as a group.

What causes these age differences in so many aspects of social and personal behavior? How permanent are these contrasts? Is it to be expected that Kirk's youthful radicalism will turn to a "slightly conservative" outlook in middle age, like his father, and "very conservative" in old age? What accounts for the fact that Johann is "very happy" in old age, despite the multiple losses he has experienced—retirement, widowerhood, and physical handicap? Throughout this essay we will be exploring such issues. First we turn to explanations for age-group differences in behavior.

DIMENSIONS OF CHANGE OVER TIME: DEVELOPMENTAL AND HISTORICAL

It is very important to remember that age, or aging, is not in itself an explanation for differences that are observed in behavior with the passage of time. *Age is only an index of events which occur at different points of time.* For example, "growing up" is our shorthand way of describing the fact that a number of events have occurred in a young person's life: attaining physical and sexual maturity, graduating from school, attaining responsible judgment. These events correspond very roughly to the passage of time—that is, the number of birthdays an individual has had. However, some people appear grown up at 16, while others may seem "immature" at 21. And "growing old" is a series of events which are even more remotely connected with chronological age. We see people who appear old at 60, while a few 75-year-olds seem more appropriately labeled "middle aged."

In examining the changes involved in growing up and growing old, therefore, it is crucial to recognize that we are talking not about chronological age but about *events* which are linked to the passage of time. Moreover, it helps to understand that two different dimensions of time are involved and, therefore, two different kinds of events. Dean Black and I have discussed these dimensions of time and events in another paper (Bengtson and Black, 1973); what follows is a very abbreviated summary of some very complex issues regarding time and behavior change (see also Riley, Johnson, and Foner, 1972; Riegel, 1969; Neugarten and Datan, 1973).

Developmental time and developmental events What we usually think about when confronted with issues of growing up and aging is *developmental time:* the individual life-cycle punctuated by events as a person celebrates (or ignores) birthday after birthday. A more common term (but one which is less precise and therefore less useful) is "maturing," a process which is seen in the unfolding biography of an individual.

If we follow a person through the course of his life we observe *changes* in everyday behavior: the way he spends his time, the way he relates to others around him, his stated goals, the concerns he expresses. But we also would see *similarity* between behavior at one point of time and another—the studious teenager becoming the preoccupied scientist, the sorority president becoming the P.T.A. chairman. In other words, the developing biography of an individual is like a motion picture: each frame represents a picture that is slightly different from the one before it, but similar enough so the pattern has continuity.

Why? What accounts for the change from one life cycle point to the next, in the continuing life of one individual? Differences in developmental time are best seen as the product of *developmental events*. These are occurrences which are experienced by most individuals during the course of life and which have some systematic influence in the ordering of human behavior. However, the order in which these events occur (indeed, whether a given event occurs at all) varies from individual to individual. This is why biographies are different for different people and why one person may "age" more rapidly than another.

It is important to recognize that developmental events may be biological, psychological, or sociological in nature. *Biological events* include the attainment and loss of reproductive capacity, the experiencing of growth and decline in physical vigor, the loss of cells and functions, and the increasing probability of disease in organs. *Psychological events* include the development of cognitive capacities, changes in the experiencing of expansion and contraction of life, and consequent changes in orientation toward future events or life goals. *Sociological events* include the entrance into and exit from the major areas of social interaction in life—marriage, work, parenting, social organizations—along with succession to greater and then lesser positions of responsibility and power within social networks or institutions.

Some of the behavioral differences evidenced in the three generations of Johnsons, therefore, can be explained by differences between the three in levels of *developmental time*—not in terms of age alone but in the various events which occur with the passage of time. This is what is often termed the *maturational effect*. Young Kirk's goals are long-range, humanitarian, and intense; his father Archie's goals are more immediate and concern his own situation; and Johann won't even talk about goals—because, in part, each of them is at a different point in the psychological dimension of developmental time. Johann discusses at great length his health, Archie casually mentions his compensating for a decline in energy, but Kirk dismisses the subject entirely—because the three differ with respect to developmental events of biology. Archie spends much of his week in an office with other people, Kirk spends only slightly less time reading textbooks and sitting in classes, and Johann has a daily program entirely of his own making—all because of differences in the sociological events associated with the work career.

Not all of the differences in their behavior can be accounted for by contrasts in developmental time or "maturation," however. Nor is it likely that Kirk will appear, at age 48, to be a carbon copy of his father in terms of general patterns of behavior. There is another dimension of time which is associated with events and which explains some of the contrasts between young, middle-aged, and elderly individuals.

Historical time and historical events: the cohort effect   It is obvious that change with the passage of time is not limited to individuals. Organizations (such as the Pasadena First Methodist church) undergo quite a turnover from decade to decade in the type of people and the kinds of activities that are prominent. Nations (such as Germany) appear very different today when compared with 1900. And civilizations (the "age of Rome") rise and wane. The metaphor of growth, development, and decline are applied to societies and groups almost as freely as these terms are used to describe the biography of an individual.

Historical time, like developmental time, has meaning only as it marks off the passage of events. Just as we use a basically meaningless chronological event (birthdays) as a shorthand way of representing developmental events, so we use an astronomical event (the rotation of the earth about the sun) as a means of counting historical time. However, we also talk about "epochs" or "periods" of history—just as we use "stages" such as adolescence, middle age, and old age to summarize sets of developmental events that seem to have some relation to each other. Periods of history are signals that, in the historian's analysis anyway, something important has changed and the society or group is different than it was earlier.

The point for our discussion is this: historical events have an impact on individual behavior. A war causes individuals not only to change their attitudes (becoming more—or less—patriotic, developing different goals) but also to change their life style (sacrificing consumer goods, joining an army). More important, the event continues to have an impact on them for a long time afterwards—perhaps for the rest of their lives. I know a man who still refuses to have anything to do with Germans (his son died in World War II) and a woman who won't keep any of her money in the bank (the bank failures during the Depression wiped out her modest savings account).

Furthermore, it stands to reason that a particular historical event has a differential impact on individuals who are of different ages. A war obviously affects the young: their careers are interrupted, they go off to fight, they become heroes, they die. The same event affects the elderly quite differently: they have seen other wars, national honor rather than personal valor is their concern, perhaps they know there are ultimately only losers in a war. The differential impact on age groups of other events is more difficult to interpret. Have American race riots caused young more than middle-aged whites to become more aware of racism and poverty? I think so; at least public opinion polls show that those under 30 in 1972 ranked "racism" as a more serious national problem than those over 30. Did the Kent State killings cause more young people than elderly to question the morality of "legal" armed retaliation against civil disobedience? I think so, judging by age differences in national opinion polls concerning this issue.

Before we go any further, it is necessary to define an important concept which has implications for any analysis of differences between age groups. An age *cohort* is a group of people who were born in the same period of historical time and who therefore are of approximately the same chronological age. The term "cohort effect" is used to describe the impact a particular historical event has on a group of individuals. When people speak of the "youth generation" what they really mean is the youth cohort (the term "generation" being probably better reserved for members of the same biological family). Note that members of the same cohort are similar with respect to the two dimensions of time and events we have just discussed: being the same age, they have experienced roughly the same developmental events, and they have lived through the same historical events. One would expect, therefore, that members of the same cohort would be similar to each other in many aspects of behavior and in some respects different from members of other cohorts.

The differences in behavior observed among the three generations of Johnsons can in part be explained in terms of historical events and the cohort effect. The fact that Johann is "very conservative" and a staunch Nixon Republican may be explained by the fact that his cohort has tended to vote for conservatives and Republicans ever since he first voted in 1922—for it is not true that people always grow more conservative with age (Cutler, 1970). The fact that Kirk is living with a girl outside marriage may be a reflection of his cohort's innovative view of man-woman relations—rather than as a youthful sowing of wild oats (which would be a "maturational" explanation). That Archie works so hard and is so concerned about his savings account may not be because middle-aged people are always more concerned about money than young people, but because Archie grew up during the Depression when his family's assets were insufficient to pay the mortgage on their farm. Such historical events (for changes in attitudes toward marriage are events just like wars and depressions) appear to have a lasting impact on individuals and explain something about the behavioral differences among age groups.

DIMENSIONS OF SOCIAL STRUCTURE: INTERPERSONAL AND INSTITUTIONAL CONTEXTS

The most distinctive characteristic of human behavior is its social nature. Before attempting to integrate all the concepts and processes presented in this discussion of time, change, and everyday behavior, we should note some dimensions of social forces at work on the developing individual as he moves through time.

Sociology may be defined as the study of the forms and processes of the behavior of human beings in relation to each other. Our concern in this paper is the way age, or events that occur with the passage of time, may influence these social forms and processes. There are two levels of analysis which can be used in examining such influence: the interpersonal context of individuals and the institutional context of society.

Both are dimensions of social organization. Before examining these two levels, we should define some elementary concepts in sociology—what may be called the building blocks of social organization. These elements are apparent at both the interpersonal and the institutional level of sociological analysis.

Elements of social organization "Social organization" refers to the pattern of interrelationships that can be observed among subunits of a human group. It refers to the *positions* or divisions of labor within the group in the carrying out of tasks; to the system of *norms* or expectations that are associated with those positions; and to the *values* (as concretely manifest in the differential status of various positions) by which decisions are made concerning alternative actions by the group. Sociologists are concerned with establishing the regularities of social organization and interaction, those processes of behavior which seem to transcend the characteristics of specific individuals that make up the group. In the analysis of age-related dimensions of social organization, the concepts of norms, roles, status, and reference groups seem to be especially useful tools.

Norms can be defined quite simply as behavioral expectations: rules concerning what is appropriate or inappropriate action in a particular situation. Almost everything we do in the course of a day is governed by some kind of these social rules. The way others view us, and to a large extent the way we view ourselves, is in a sense a function of how well we live up to these norms. Norms are enforced by *sanctions,* which are actions having the effect of rewarding conformity to the expected behavior or punishing departures from expected behavior. Sanctions can be either external (the approval or censure from other people) or internal (feelings of guilt or shame which themselves are social products).

Norms are socially defined; even the precepts of divine revelation are mediated by men. Norms vary in the degree to which they are shared (not everyone feels that stealing stamps from the company one works for is wrong) and in the degree to which they are enforced (some norms are institutionalized into "laws," departure from which may result in an unwanted sojourn in prison). Because they are socially defined they are subject to change. Examples of the above are numerous. There are norms which say a student should attend class, that a barmaid should report tips for income tax, that a driver should signal his intention to turn, that a man should open the door for a woman (who, nowadays, just might feel slightly insulted if he does). Norms, therefore, represent tenuous operating agreements which are negotiated and elaborated by specific actors in specific situations. However, their influence is so pervasive on everyday behavior that they are probably the most important system of variables for social scientists to take into account (Goffman, 1966).

Roles may be defined as behaviors assigned to a particular position in the carrying out of a task. As in the theater, roles are parts that are played out in the enactment of some theme. Obviously roles are related to norms—that is, they tell us how to play the part appropriately and what others expect of us in a given scene. One is expected to do certain things as a father, as a husband, as an employee, and as a Rotarian. An individual functions simultaneously in many roles or positions in the course of a day, and this may lead to *interrole* conflict, as when your son's Indian Guides outing conflicts with your Rotarian meeting. There may be many roles associated with a given position. As a married woman one must be a chauffeur, hostess, lover, chef, playmate, therapist, and business manager. Such a long list of expectations associated with a particular social position might create *intra-*role conflict.

I prefer to define *status* as the relative rank of a person or position in a group; it may also be defined as the prestige, honor, or worth attached to a position. Status accrues to an individual to the extent that he possesses something that is valued by the group. In America status is associated primarily with characteristics that are achieved—and that achievement is usually defined in terms of economic production (translated simply into money). Thus occupation, education, and income are valued characteristics that determine status in our society—but so is age or sex, attributes that are ascribed rather than achieved. In our production-oriented society, youth is more highly valued than is old age, and so is being male rather than female. As will be discussed later, these status criteria associated with aging have important consequences in everyday behavior.

Status as a dimension of social organization is related to roles in that some roles have higher status than others. Also, holding a high-status position on one dimension is often an entry criterion for other high-status positions. Status is related to norms in that expectations for behavior vary depending on the rank of the individual in society. We expect adults to be more responsible than children, public officials to be more civic-minded than ordinary citizens, females to be less aggressive than males, old people less assertive than young ones.

Finally, *reference groups* are those sets of others, present or symbolic, which serve as standards for an individual's behavior and with which he identifies. In short, they serve as a source for his norms and values. The delinquent gang member, for example, breaks the norms of middle-class society—risking harsh legal sanctions of that society—because the perspective of his reference group provides other standards of behavior. Whenever I speak to an audience of Rotarians or a Junior Chamber of Commerce group I'm struck by how much the university community serves as my reference group: not only do I see an entirely different standard of dress employed at the businessman's luncheon meeting, but the humor, the topics of conversation, and my own evaluation of whether I've done a good job are entirely at variance with the standards of my academic peers. That audience becomes a temporary reference group for me. But when I get back to the classroom I take off my tie, tell puns instead of bawdy stories, and drop footnotes to other scholars instead of relating sociology to the financial pages.

Age and the interpersonal context The "micro-level" of sociological analysis involves examining the social environment of a given individual. We are interested in describing how the individual interacts with the many kinds of others he meets in the usual course of daily activity, and what meaning these interactions have for him.

As an individual progresses through the life-cycle his interpersonal world changes. This point has often been neglected in sociological analysis. The person moves from one social position to another—from bachelor to husband to father to grandfather—and as he does the number, kind, and quality of interpersonal contacts change. These changes over time in the immediate social environment can be analyzed in terms of events that alter roles, norms, and reference groups.

The interpersonal network of an individual (friends, relatives, coworkers, neighbors, members of one's church or bowling team) can be examined at the "micro-level" in terms of activity, satisfaction, and involvement in the role. For example, Havighurst et al. (1969) studied dimensions of role activity of retired men from six different nations. They found substantial cultural differences in the profile across the entire set of roles of such dimensions of role behavior (see Bengtson, Chiriboga, and Keller, 1969).

Age and the institutional context The interpersonal context of behavior derives much of its structure from larger forces operating on interactional situations. The social positions we take in the course of our daily lives relate to functions in large part defined by the broader society. If we stop at the interpersonal level of analysis (as much research in social psychology does) we may miss seeing the forest for the trees.

The "macro-level" of sociological analysis takes a much wider focus: how large aggregates of human beings organize themselves over time in order to maintain the group's survival. Cultures, nations, and clubs exhibit patterns of organization which may be very explicit or quite unconscious. But this organization reflects the tasks that must be carried out for survival, the processes used to recruit people to carry out these tasks, and the values used to make decisions about which tasks are most important. For example, certain requirements are necessary for the maintenance of any society: the procreation and training of young; the production of food, tools, and services; the protection of individual rights within the group. There are formal groups charged with specialization in these functions: the family; the educational establishment (in complex societies); the economy; the political and legal order. These are termed the "social institutions."

Age is an important dimension of the institutional context of social life. In the first place, some institutions are concerned only with people in a given age range—education in America remains preoccupied with the very young, for example, and the economic functions of our society are controlled mostly by the middle-aged. In the second place, as an individual moves through the life-cycle his position in the institutional context of society changes. Within the economic institution, for example, a man may move from student to apprentice to journeyman to retiree. In terms of responsibility and power in most institutions there is a general progression over the life-cycle. If you were to graph the average woman's power in the family institution, you would probably find a low level in the teenage years, a great rise in the twenties and a plateau in the mid-thirties and forties, then a decline as her children are "launched" until, perhaps, she is in fact dependent on her offspring at the end of life.

Summary Using the two dimensions of social structure and examining change with the passage of the two dimensions of time (developmental and historical), we can understand many aspects of human aging and of behavioral differences among age groups. It is important to remember that age is not in itself an explanation for such differences but only an index of events which occur at different points of time.

Age is, however, a major dimension of social organization, seen in both the interpersonal and the institutional contexts. As an individual constructs his own biography in progressing through the life-cycle, his social world changes. Developmental events are associated with the manner in which he fits into the social forms and processes of the broader social institutions in which he plays a role; as he moves from one social position to another the number, kind, and quality of interpersonal contact changes. In short, the passage of time brings many developmental events in the social structure within which an individual plays out the course of his life.

2   Aging and the Social System

In Section One it was suggested that age can be seen as an index of events which occur at different points of time. We saw that maturational effects (developmental events) and cohort effects (historical events) can explain much about why the behavior of a 23-year-old is different from that of his 73-year-old grandfather. We defined some of the basic units of social structure and saw some ways in which age is a dimension of social organization, seen in both the interpersonal and the institutional contexts. It was suggested that the everyday behavior of humans, as they structure their lives and interact with each other, can be seen as the product of the interplay of various events, both external to the individual (social system) and internal (personal system).

In this section we take a closer look at age-related changes in the social system which result in both continuity and change in an individual's biography. The focus will be on growing old, for—although this has been a rather neglected area of sociological analysis—we can see quite clearly the impact of developmental events in elderly individuals. First we will look at the concept of social age, then at socialization, and finally at research related to norms, roles, status, and reference groups in the sociology of adult development and aging.

SOCIAL AGE AND DEVELOPMENTAL TIME

Defining age usually seems such a simple task: one merely counts birthdays or groups individuals into cohorts (e.g., the "Geritol set"). As was stated earlier, however, chronological age is an arbitrary yardstick that is often meaningless in characterizing functions. When one attempts to analyze everyday behavior as it changes with age, it soon becomes apparent that there are social, as well as biological, psychological, and historical, time-clocks which serve as measuring devices and which influence behavior. In this sense *age can best be defined as the cumulation of developmental events at a particular point of time in the life of an individual.*

In this section we are focusing on social events and their impact on individuals. Therefore another definition is in order, one which specifically embodies the dimensions of social structure outlined earlier. Let us say, then, that *social age refers to the rights and duties which accrue by virtue of seniority in a particular position* (Cain, 1964: 287; Neugarten and Moore, 1968: 5). These are, after all, the implications of cumulative developmental events for social behavior; they are also the social cues by virtue of which people come to be regarded as young, middle aged, or old.

We see this social definition of age in everyday circumstances. In the first place, people react to others more on the basis of the statuses or positions they have (e.g., chairman, chief of staff, executive) than with regard to their actual years. The deference accorded an Admiral is related to his seniority, which may or may not be related to his age. Of course, we react to symbolic cues that are associated with biological aging (such as wrinkled skin, a bald head) but even these are only inexactly related to chronological age. In the second place, as Linton (1940) and Wood (1971) have pointed out, such age-status patterns are more pervasive and significant than we usually acknowledge in ordering interpersonal behavior. Such positions are related to time in that people are called upon to occupy a fairly orderly succession of statuses in various areas of life as they age. However, although such age-related positions usually are roughly correlated with chronological age, often they are not.

For example, in the medical profession a man may be socially "mature" at chronological age 30, having rapidly gone through medical training and residencies; or he may be an "immature" intern at 35 if he entered medical school late. How he is treated by colleagues and patients depends more on his social age than on his chronological age. Or, consider the difference between the kind of behavior one expects of a 60-year-old who has retired, and a man of the same age who has not. In terms of many kinds of social expectations, the former is "old," the latter is not. For researchers studying the course of aging, the yardstick of social expectations may be more relevant than age measured by birthdays.

There are several implications of this usage of the term age which must be kept in mind. First, in discussing the behavioral characteristics of age groups, or in charting changes in behavior over time, one must always pay attention to the relevant comparison group, social position, or institution used in defining the variable age. All too often gerontologists discuss "the aged" in terms of all persons over age 65, without reference to the substantial individual differences in self-categorization or group reference which may make such gross generalizations inappropriate. The aged are *not* a homogeneous group; chronological age is only an imperfect approximation of social or personal age. What we need is a more precise method of determining the social punctuation points of the life-cycle as they affect individual behavior. This involves more research on the characteristic "developmental events" (as was discussed in Section One) and on the average timing of these life events in populations of individuals. Moreover, we should recognize that social definitions of age and its importance in patterning individual behavior vary greatly from one culture or social setting to another (see Clark, 1967).

Second, from the standpoint of research, age must be considered both as an independent and as a dependent variable. On the one hand the researcher must consider what behavior varies and is constrained during the course of the life-cycle; on the other hand, he must describe how people define age socially and what they perceive as the punctuation points of the lifeline.

Third, in charting the course of individuals through the social punctuation points of the life span, there often occurs what Leonard Cain (1964:287) calls "asynchronization": differences in the timing of events in various areas of one individual's life. Consider, for example, a 55-year-old steelworker whom I once interviewed. He had just retired and thus had reached the status of "old age" in the occupational or economic institution. Within the context of the family, however, he was relatively "young," for he had a 13-year-old daughter. In terms of formal voluntary organizations he was "middle aged," having just succeeded to the third most honorific position in a fraternal order. By what standards should this man's social age be calculated? In which age category does he belong? Such a question would be trivial, were it not for his own anxiety and confusion about his age status:

> I'm glad to be through with work because I couldn't take it any more. But now my friends don't know what to call me. They kid me about being an old man, and I don't feel it . . . . My wife doesn't know what to do with me, says I get underfoot being around the house all the time. . . . I guess I've got to find something to do. A man my age shouldn't just sit around.

Fourth, and most importantly, social age is relevant because it suggests some guidelines for how we should *behave.* In the example just cited, the steelworker isn't so much confused over his *age,* as over what a person his age who doesn't work should *do.* The importance of age (as socially defined at least) in patterning everyday interaction resides in the expectations it creates regarding appropriate behavior. This point will be expanded in detail when we consider "age norms" later.

One final point is crucial regarding the definition of "old age." The above discussion would appear academic except for the way in which our society adheres to a chronological definition of age to the exclusion of all others. Many tensions arise from the fact that "old age" is defined to begin at age 65 in most occupations, and thus, despite considerations of biological and psychological capacity, to say nothing of social competence, a chronological definition of aging is paramount. One thus sees in the real world many tensions that arise from conflicting criteria of age. With the increased push toward earlier retirement, greater longevity, private pension plans, and better health characterizing the American population, age 65 is increasingly proving to be an arbitrary and less than useful way to mark the "old age" stage of life.

SOCIALIZATION AND THE SOCIAL SYSTEM

The central theme of this essay is that the interplay between the individual and the social system is a constantly unfolding process, reflecting developmental and historical events as the individual moves through time. A central message of this section is that the social system—as the person experiences it—is not a static entity but reflects both continuity and change. The biography of an individual can be seen in daily and long-term confrontation with the social structure in which he lives, reflecting the new roles, the new norms, the new reference groups which characterize different points of the life-cycle.

What is the process by which the individual negotiates these changes in his social system through time? The term most often used to characterize this adaptation to change is *socialization,* which may be defined as *the learning of new behaviors and orientations as one moves into new positions in the social structure.*

It is useful to recognize that there are two perspectives on the analysis of socialization and its mechanisms. On the one hand, social scientists study the *efforts of the social system and its institutions* (often called "socialization agents") to prepare the individual for his new role. This is seen in studies of the behavior of parents; of the organization of educational institutions; of the procedures of prisons, mental hospitals, and military boot camps. On the other hand, researchers study the *processes in the individual* (often called the "socializee") by which he learns these new roles and adapts to the new expectations. Such terms as imitation and modeling, identification and internalization are often used in such analyses, but these terms do injustice to the active restructuring that the individual usually engages in when moving into a new position. Also, it should be recognized that people often create new positions or carry out an established position in a novel way. Perhaps the best way to characterize this process is a "transformation of identity" (Strauss, 1969) which connotes the fact that the individual who has moved into a new position has a new outlook, new sets of skills, which spill over into other social positions.

At any rate, socialization should properly be regarded as a *continuous bilateral negotiation between the individual and the social system as he moves into new positions through time.* Both the goals and efforts of the social system and the individual's active integration of the new roles and expectations should be kept in mind (Bengtson and Black, 1973).

Socialization is most obvious during childhood, that period of most obvious acquisition of the necessities of social behavior. One must learn to hold one's bowels, to say "please," to talk only at specified instances in class, to comb one's hair in a certain way; the list is endless. It is similarly true, but somewhat less obvious, that socialization occurs throughout the life-cycle. Whenever one moves into a different social position there are many new behaviors which must be learned in order to fill that position acceptably. However, there are important differences between early and later socialization (Brim, 1966). In childhood one is helped and even forced to learn the new behaviors by agencies of socialization: the family which teaches good manners, the school which teaches normatively correct expression in writing and speaking as well as values such as "citizenship."

In adulthood one finds few agencies to program individual behavior into ways acceptable to new positions. (There are exceptions to this, such as boot camp or medical school, but these pertain to very specialized positions and very specific periods of life.) This is what makes the normal transitions of adulthood—that is, the role changes—so difficult in our society. How does one learn the behaviors which are necessary in order to become a good mother? a happy retiree? a valued grandfather? a graceful widow? The questions just posed reflect some of the fundamental problems in the natural course of adulthood and aging. For the social scientist interested in the study of aging these problems are translated into more general terms: How does the social system change for individuals as they move into the later phases of the life-cycle, and how may socialization into the positions which are usually associated with old age be characterized?

Social age and age grading   First, let us return again to the issue of age as a dimension of social organization and see what divisions of the adult life-cycle are commonly made by our society. As was suggested earlier, aging in the everyday interactional world is socially defined; to be "old" or "elderly" is to have reached some social milestone. The term *age grading* refers to these age positions and the system developed by a culture to give order and predictability to the life course followed by individuals (Wood, 1971:75). It is implied that individuals undergo a process of behavior change as they move into new age grades. The freshman in college defines himself and behaves differently than he did three months earlier as a senior in high school because he occupies a different position, different things are expected of him, and his behavior is judged accordingly. Is there such a clear-cut differentiation in adult-hood? When does old age, or middle age for that matter, begin? Just what are the indications of passage from one age grade to the next in adulthood?

Professor Bernice Neugarten and her associates at the University of Chicago have carried out a series of inquiries concerning age status.

> The points along the life-line at which the individual moves from "child" to "adolescent" to "adult" are socially defined, although they are timed in close relation to biological development. After physical maturity is reached, social age continues to be marked off by relatively clear cut biological or social events in the family cycle. Thus marriage marks the end of one social age period and the beginning of another; as does the appearance of the first child, the departure of children from the home, and the birth of children's children. At each stage, the individual takes on new roles, and his prestige is altered in relation to other family members. At each of these points he may be said to occupy a new position within the age-status system of the family (Neugarten and Moore, 1968: 6).

Several studies point both to the reality of age grading in adulthood in our society and to the way in which age grading is differentially defined according to the socioeconomic status of individuals. Neugarten and Peterson (1957) report a study of 240 men and women, age 40-70, in a metropolitan Midwestern area. Their sample was stratified by age, sex, and social class. They found a general consensus concerning four periods of the life-cycle: "young adulthood" (20 to about 30); "maturity" (30 to 40); "middle age" (40 to 60); and "old age" (the period after sixty). Old age appears to be defined as occurring slightly later by older respondents and earlier for younger ones. What is more significant is the degree to which social class differences emerged in their sample. For example, men perceived 30 as being the major dividing point in the life-cycle, women, 40; the upper middle class respondents tended to divide the lifeline at 30, 40, and 65, while those from the lowest social class defined the dividing points at 25, 35, and 50. This may reflect the fact that working class individuals reach their peak of occupational status and income earlier, and the rate at which they move through adult careers (work as well as family—Spence and Lonner, 1971) is accelerated compared to the middle class.

Age-status systems, since they are socially defined, vary according to cultural and historical conditions. For example, there have been dramatic shifts in population distributions by age since 1900, in that a larger proportion of our population is middle aged and elderly today. In addition to these data on the numbers of individuals in various age groups, it is interesting to examine the shifts in the way the life-cycle is punctuated by historical changes—for example, in timing of events in American families since the turn of the century (Glick, Heer, and Beresford, 1959). From Table 1, it can be seen that in 70 years the median age of marriage has dropped two years; birth of the last child has dropped five years; marriage of the last child has dropped eight years; and the duration of marriage has increased ten years. It is interesting

Table 1.   Median age of husband and wife at successive events in the family cycle

Stage	1890	1940	1950	1959	1980
Median age of wife at—					
First marriage	22.0	21.5	20.1	20.2	19.5-20.4
Birth of last child*	31.9	27.1	26.1	25.8	27-28
Marriage of last child	55.3	50.0	47.6	47.1	48-49
Death of husband	53.3	60.9	61.4	63.6	65-66
Median age of husband at—					
First marriage	26.1	24.3	22.8	22.3	22-23
Birth of last child	36.0	29.9	28.8	27.9	29-30
Marriage of last child	59.4	52.8	50.3	49.2	51-52
Death of wife	57.4	63.6	64.1	65.7	68-69

*The authors suggest that these ages are probably too young by a year or two for all dates, according to data from cohorts of women collected in August, 1959, by the Bureau of Census.

Source: Glick, Heer, and Beresford, 1959.

also to note social class differences in such timing. From other data (Neugarten and Moore, 1968) it appears that the greater the education, the later these punctuation points appear. Also, the ordering of early events—schooling, marriage, and parenthood—has changed for the present generation of young people. Increasingly, more students are marrying while still in school.

What is more important to emphasize, however, is

> . . . the clear implication that the timing of the family cycle is not only biologically regulated, but socially regulated; that social expectations become differentiated among different socioeconomic groups; and that these expectations are reflected in behavior—in this case, in the overall regularity of time intervals between family events (Neugarten and Moore, 1968: 8).

In the economic sphere there are other indications of a changing age-status system in our country. Economic maturity—that is, work force participation—has become greatly truncated over the past decades. Men enter the labor force later and leave sooner than ever before. For women, a new pattern of economic participation has begun to emerge, with women in their 50s joining women in their 20s as participants in the labor force.

> The timing, then, of immaturity, maturity, and post-maturity in economic terms has clearly altered over the past decades. Indeed, changes in these respects are so fundamental that they have led, along with related changes of social age within the family, to the broad redefinitions of age groups that may be said to have emerged in America over the past 50 years as adolescents, on the one hand, and the aged, on the other, have been set apart as special groups in the society (Neugarten and Moore, 1968: 11-12).

Age norms That there are social (and historical) as well as biological time clocks is indicated by the research just reviewed. Moreover, it seems that individuals are quite aware of the normative qualities associated with the gathering of birthdays. They are aware that there are expectations concerning appropriate behavior at various ages:

> Age norms and age expectations operate as prods and brakes upon behavior, in some instances hastening an event, in others delaying it. Men and women . . . are aware also of their own timing and readily describe themselves as "early," "late" or "on time" with regard to family and occupational events. Age norms also operate in many less clear-cut ways and in more peripheral areas of adult life as illustrated in such phrases as, "He's too old to be working so hard" or "She's too young to wear that style of clothing" or "That's a strange thing for a man of his age to say" (Neugarten, Moore, and Lowe, 1965: 711).

Age norms are enforced by a variety of sanctions, not the least effective of which is the admonition to "Act your age!" Neugarten and her associates present data to indicate that, despite the great diversity of things in the social environment that influence attitudes, a substantial consensus exists concerning age norms for behavior. In several samples of men and women of various ages, social classes, and ethnic groups, a similar pattern of age norms emerged (see Wood, 1971).

The importance of age-specific norms in ordering individual behavior may increase with age. Neugarten, Moore, and Lowe (1965) and Wood

(1971) report that older respondents seem more aware of the relevance and validity of age-appropriate behavior. They perceive greater age constraints on behavior than do young people.

> This age-related difference in point of view is perhaps well illustrated by the response of a twenty-year-old, when asked what he thought of marriage between seventeen-year-olds, said, "I suppose it would be all right. . . . Why not? It isn't age that's the important thing." A forty-five-year-old, by contrast, said, "At that age they'd be foolish. . . . Kids who marry that young will suffer for it later." (Neugarten, Moore, and Lowe, 1965: 716)

In this study, respondents were asked to indicate "your own opinion" and "other peoples' opinion" regarding 39 items of behavior. (To give an example, "A woman feels it's all right at her age to wear a two-piece bathing suit: when she's 45 (approve/disapprove); 30 (approve/disapprove); 18 (approve/disapprove)." They found that age is a more salient criterion to older judges than to younger ones in evaluating the appropriateness of an individual's behavior.

Norms in old age The preceding discussion indicates that age norms, or definitions of behavior appropriate at designated ages, are an important determinant of the manner of social interaction. However, there are other aspects of the relationship between behavioral expectancies and the passage of time which should be considered. Does the *content* of norms differ in middle and old age? Are there specific expectations associated with the age status of being "elderly"? To what degree do norms actually operate as constraints on individual behavior in old age? In sum, how can we specify what values and behaviors people are expected to have simply by virtue of being old?

Relatively little research has been carried out on these questions (see the excellent review by Rosow, 1973). One of the pioneer studies concerning social aspects of aging still contains more relevant data than any other investigation on this topic. Havighurst and Albrecht (1953) studied attitude and activity patterns in 1949 and 1951 in a small community called "Prairie City." In the section of their study designed to tap norms concerning behavior in old age, they presented 128 items of possible behaviors for old people (for example: spending time in a tavern with old friends, making speculative investments, interacting frequently with younger people). These were submitted for public approval/disapproval scores to a sample of adults of various ages. Their results indicated that there is very little evidence for the existence of norms specifically built around old age. Most of the things that were highly approved reflected the basic values of the local culture applicable to all adults, not simply to the aged.

What activities were most highly approved for older people? Accepting minor civic responsibilities; voting regularly; keeping in regular touch with friends and relatives by visit or mail; maintaining an active special interest or hobby; being actively involved with the church; and pursuing an active social life in the community, especially among persons one's own age.

What are the few age-specific expectations—norms that are applicable specifically to the aged? They focus on income maintenance, the family, and the church. Older people should be more interested in religion and the church than they previously were. They should be greatly interested in their grandchildren and great-grandchildren and should maintain ritual contact with their children at definite times, especially during holidays. But otherwise they should lead a life separate from their children. Finally, they should maintain financial independence as long as possible, primarily through work.

What behaviors are strongly disapproved for elderly individuals? These norms follow similar patterns, again focusing on general rather than age-specific standards. The general prescriptions condemn a life of isolation and inactivity, solitude, the frequent violation of generational interaction barriers, and inattention to religion. The authors suggest that two conclusions can be drawn from this study:

> First, it seems clear that a wide variety of activities that are approved for people in middle age are also generally approved for older people. The major exception to this blanket approval of adult activities for older people is the disapproval of over activity for older people, of older people acting like young adults, and of older people attempting to continue activities without letup from the peak reached at middle age.
>
> Second, this study shows that people in their young adult and middle years are generally more approving of activity for older people than the old people themselves. The "approval scores" for most activities in the questionnaire were higher from people in the young or middle years than they were from people past 70 (Havighurst and Albrecht, 1953: 36).

It should be obvious that norms are highly dependent on cultural values and sociohistorical conditions. The Havighurst and Albrecht study was based on a sample from a small town twenty years ago. Thus a study carried out today, based on a national and representative sample, might afford quite different conclusions concerning norms associated with old age. Nevertheless, all available evidence points to the following conclusions: (a) there are very few norms regarding appropriate or inappropriate behavior which are specific to old age; (b) the norms that are cited have to do with maintaining independence, social activity, and religiosity—in other words, goals appropriate to middle age—in the face of biological decline (for similar conclusions, see Clark, 1967; Wood, 1971).

Normlessness in old age: negative and positive consequences We have seen that the matrix of norms regarding appropriate behavior appears to become less salient with the passage of developmental time in later maturity. Though age-grading systems in our society do define a period of "old age," and though older people in particular are conscious that earlier behaviors are somehow no longer appropriate, there is very little evidence of clearly defined and widely shared expectations concerning what people should do during this period of life. One aspect of the change in the individual's social system with the passage of time, therefore, is that there are fewer and fewer clear-cut obligations of appropriate behavior as one passes into the socially defined stage of "old age."

What are the consequences of this increase in "normlessness" in later maturity? Most analyses in social gerontology have focused on the negative implications of the increasing lack of normative restraints on individual action (see Kuypers and Bengtson, 1973). Durkheim long ago pointed to the tie between "normlessness" and individual disruption (alienation, leading to suicide) or social disruption (anomie, revolution, or anarchy). Rosow has consistently argued that this normlessness puts the aged in a weakened position:

> . . . the norms provide no set of expectations that effectively structure an older person's activities and roles and abstract his pattern of life. . . . The anomaly for the aged is that with amorphous norms, there are few criteria for conformity or deviance, for success or failure. Hence, there are few bases for allocating either rewards or punishments. . . . This in itself is a significant discontinuity in life that intensifies the weakness of motives for becoming old. It also heavily underscores the fact that the social consequences of older peoples' performance is relatively insignificant and that the society has little stake in their attitudes or behavior (Rosow, 1973: 39,40).

As we have seen, an old person's life is conspicuously lacking in social norms for relationships outside the family. As was noted earlier, almost everything we do in the course of the day is governed by some kind of social norms. The way others view us, and the way we view ourselves, is in a sense a function of how well we live up to these norms. Thus it appears that one consequence of the decreased normative constraints in later maturity would be uncertainty and alienation (Martin, Bengtson, and Acock, 1973).

There is, however, another interpretation. Decrease in specific social requirements and expectations can also be interpreted as a gain in *freedom.* I would argue that the loss of norms (and roles with which they are associated) represents a potential *opportunity* to pick and choose among alternative behaviors—a degree of freedom from societal restraints that is perhaps greater than at any other period of the life-cycle. One often hears about the negative consequences of normlessness in old age: what I am suggesting is that this decrease in normative specificity also implies freedom to those who choose (and have the capability) to exploit it.

The point has been stated differently by a number of investigators who suggest that social norms become more flexible and liberal with advancing age, allowing actors a progressively greater range of personal choice in structuring their lives. Cumming and Henry, for example, report from their sample of 80-year-olds that:

> These very old people seem inwardly directed; all their energy is spent in one form or another on self-concern, without interference from the social norms that once forced them to consider others. On the other hand, our seventy-year-olds still seem to be in the process of being freed from these norms, and they reveal it by giving normative responses resembling those (of younger age groups) . . . (Cumming and Henry, 1961: 204).

Neugarten (1965b) has characterized this process as the "greater interiority of experiencing." Martin, Bengtson, and Acock (1973) found that older individuals had lower levels of alienation (including normlessness) than the young adults in the sample. Rosow has emphasized the tie between the decreased saliency of norms and role loss (which will be discussed in the next section) in the following way:

> . . . as people age, the limitation of their responsibilities and power sharply reduces their ability to affect others adversely and thereby the significant social consequences of their behavior. . . . There is less social stake in their behavior and correspondingly little concern with the options that older people exercise and the choices they make . . . more alternatives are available to them in the sphere of their own private lives. So long as they do not become a burden to others or indulge in virtually bizarre behavior, within their means they can do very largely as they want and live as they wish (Rosow, 1973: 36,37).

Some support for this theme of the potentially positive consequences of lessened normative constraint also comes from the Cornell Study of Occupational Retirement. Streib and Schneider (1971) suggest that the very normlessness of old age may be advantageous to the older person whose declining energy makes it difficult to meet specific demands of society.

Age roles, stereotypes, and role loss in old age The preceding section suggested that there are two aspects to the question of norms and age: age-graded norms, or the ways in which things are deemed appropriate or inappropriate at various ages; and norms regarding old age, or behaviors prescribed by society for individuals in the latter phase of the life-cycle. Similarly there are two aspects to the question of roles and age. The first has to do with the existence of a generalized role position in our social structure which can be termed the "role of the aged." This question gets us into a consideration of age stereotypes. The second has to do with the way in which performance in the common roles of adult life—friend, father, spouse—changes with advancing years.

In terms of the first issue, it seems generally clear that it is not useful to talk about old age as a generalized role. Yet, as Rosow (1973) has pointed out, gerentologists have often blithely assumed that there is a distinctive role for older people and a specifiable set of beliefs and actions that is expected of the aged. One reason for this may be the pervasiveness of stereotypes regarding the aged.

Stereotypes can be defined as widely shared expectancies, without specific sanctions, regarding the behavior or characteristics of a particular category of people. Thus the stereotype of a Black man in the American South until recently was of an individual who, in addition to having dark skin, could be expected to be lazy, childish, and submissive. The stereotype of an Oriental is someone who is quiet, tidy, thrifty, and clannish. There are stereotypes about "masculine" and "feminine" behavior. The distinctive thing about such expectations is that they do not acknowledge individual differences among those who are members of that social category. Furthermore, these inaccurate over-generalizations, often acquired on the basis of limited contact with the group, are usually (but not exclusively) negative, associated with some sort of stigma. Stereotypes are, therefore, overgeneralization of social positions (roles) that have vague and often inaccurate expectancies associated with them.

That there are stereotypes about the aged has been well documented (McTavish, 1971; Hickey and Kalish, 1968; Palmore, 1971). The attitudes of young people about the old are often stereotypic. Frequently, aging individuals accept such stereotypes, so that their own expectations concerning aging are inaccurate. Based on information about the small group of institutionalized elderly, for example, the erroneous generalization may be made that most persons over the age of seventy have "senile" qualities. Similarly it is often assumed that the elderly are politically conservative, or lacking in sexual interest and motivation, or that they are more religious than younger people, or that they dread death (Seltzer and Atchley, 1971). Moreover, as Atchley has noted:

> *From a purely practical point of view, old age itself is a stigma. . . . By far the most important aspect . . . is its negative, disqualifying character. On the basis of their age, older people are usually relegated to a position in society in which they are no longer judged to be of any use or importance. Like most other expendable elements in society, older people are subjected to poverty, illness, and social isolation (Atchley, 1972: 14).*

These attitudes about the elderly *in general* are false; but they persist in stereotypic thinking. From stereotypes about a category of persons to expectancies regarding an individual member's behavior is a small step indeed; and this is one reason why it is often naively assumed that there *is* a "role of the elderly" in our society. It seems to me it would be best to omit entirely any reference to the "role" of members of a particular age group.

Concerning the way in which performance in the common roles of adult life change with advancing years, much more can be said. From

27

research by Havighurst and Albrecht (1953), Maddox (1963), Rosow (1968), Palmore (1968), and others, it seems quite clear that the social world of aging individuals changes, usually contracting with the passage of time. The number and kind of social contacts decreases; roles are literally lost as retirement, widowhood, the death of friends, and decreasing physical mobility leave the individual increasingly to his own resources. This may be viewed as a shrinkage of roles. There is also a general decrease in overall social activity with advancing years.

There also occurs a decrease in activity in specific roles, though this decrease is selective. Data from a cross-national study of aging (Bengtson, 1969) indicate that men in their seventies usually display a general pattern of very low activity in roles such as club member, civic/political participant, and church member; a slightly higher pattern of activity in the roles of friend, neighbor, and acquaintance; and the highest activity in family roles such as parent and grandparent. The change-in-activity patterns, determined by comparisons with the subject's role activity at age 60, mirror this trend. There is significant decrease in activity in the roles outside the family, but not in family roles per se.

In summary, there are two aspects of role change which affect the social system of individuals as they move into old age. The first is the role ambiguity associated with moving into the status of "old age"—there is no clearly defined position having associated with it expectancies and taboos. The second is the shrinkage of role repertoires and the decreased activity in roles outside the family. The personal consequences of these role changes will be discussed in Section Three.

Old age and reference groups Passage from one age status to the next at earlier points in the life-cycle is often accompanied by a change in reference groups. The first-year medical student takes as the standard for judging his behavior his new medical school classmates, not the fraternity or undergraduate groups which formerly served as his referent. Such reference group influences are pervasive at various points of the life span; for instance, many writers have pointed to a "subculture of youth" in our society. Indeed, one implication of the currently fashionable "generation gap" debate is that cohorts of individuals born in different periods take their own age group as referents to the exclusion of other age groups, resulting in a psychological chasm between them (Bengtson, 1970,1971).

It may be said that individuals moving into old age, especially as they retire, are restructuring their social definition of themselves; but to what extent is this accompanied by a change of reference groups? To what extent is there a group consciousness among the aged, as there is in the "Now Generation"?

This issue has been hotly debated by sociologists in the field of aging in recent years, but little evidence has been accumulated of anything approaching a subculture of the aged (Streib, 1965; Rosow, 1973; Palmore and Whittington, 1971; Trela, 1971). Arnold Rose (1965) has argued that there is evolving a sense of group consciousness among aged individuals —involving political action, a sense of group pride, and a desire to associate with age peers to the exclusion of younger people. His findings, however, seem to apply only to an extremely limited number of older people; it is difficult to see how, except in a very general sense, the majority of older people look to their peers as a reference group furnishing standards by which to judge appropriate behavior. The reference group for the elderly seems more correctly to be people in their middle years.

The reason for this is implied in the foregoing discussion of roles, norms, and statuses. In passing from middle to old age one loses much of the *achieved* statuses that accompany the roles of mid-life: status as a member of a particular occupation, as breadwinner, as mother to dependent children. The aging individual moves to a position characterized by *ascribed* status; just on the basis of having gathered so many birthdays, one is "old" (Streib and Schneider, 1971). As has been indicated, there are few norms associated with this status. Thus one looks back to the middle years for guides to behavior. For the first time in one's life, perhaps, one has no age-appropriate reference group (Rosow, 1973). An exception to this may be seen in participation in Senior Citizens organizations (Trela, 1971) but there is little evidence of "group consciousness" in significant numbers of elderly individuals.

The social system and adult socialization In concluding this section we must return to the concept of socialization and its part in assisting the individual to deal with age-related changes in social positions. Socialization can be seen as the bridge between social system changes (as the individual moves from one age-related position to another) and personal system adjustments. The function of socialization, it was suggested earlier, is to prepare an individual for new positions within the everchanging social system. Socialization may then be viewed from two quite different perspectives: (a) the effort of the social system to prepare the individual for status change; (b) "transformations of identity"—the personal internalization by the individual of the new position with its associated group of expectations, and the person's active restructuring of that role.

There are fewer and fewer indications of the social system's organized effort in preparing individuals for the new positions they assume with advancing years. Consider, for example, the general and somewhat vague age-grade change of becoming "old." Sometime between the sixth and seventh decades an individual comes to be regarded (and, in turn, comes to regard himself) as no longer being "middle aged." "Old age" is a devalued status in our society; that is, the position "old person" has less social value than the position "middle-aged person" (Parsons, 1942). Thus there is no explicit social reward for moving into the status of "old"—unless you like the idea of freedom from the responsibilities of middle age. It is not surprising to note that, though the passage from youth to adulthood is marked by many institutional arrangements—legal, interpersonal, occupational—no such socialization experiences characterize the transition from middle to old age.

In the role change termed "retirement," to give a more clear-cut example, there may be no formal or ceremonial leave-taking of the role of worker, nor is there much formal socialization for nonwork in the usual set of work experiences. Maddox remarks that "For most employees . . . this significant transition appears to be unceremonious, perhaps almost intentionally so, as though retirement were an event which one does not wish to mark especially" (Maddox, 1966:118). Of course, there may be specific career style factors that affect the possibility of socialization for retirement life; for example, it has been suggested that the occupation of the teacher provides some "rehearsal for retirement" along the life-cycle, as contrasted with the career of industrial workers (Bengtson, Chiriboga, and Keller, 1969). Moreover, retirement preparation programs are becoming common, and several studies have shown that they have positive consequences (for an excellent review see Atchley, 1972: 159). In any event retirement is a signal that one is aged (in social terms), and this has immediate consequences for the individual.

For the aging female, the role change evidenced by widowhood is common: most married women will be widows during a significant portion of their lives (Riley, Foner, and associates, 1968: 987). Here we find an even greater lack of any kind of institutional preparation on the part of the social system for role change. (In terms of psychological process, though, Neugarten has suggested that there may be an intrapsychic or fantasy-level "rehearsal for widowhood" as the middle-aged woman finds her friends experiencing this role loss.)

In the role change represented by the leave-taking of grown children there is somewhat more evidence of socialization (Deutscher, 1964). This is true, however, simply because the focus of growing children's interaction is progressively less within the framework of the home—not because of any social system provisions for the role change. In fact, the "empty nest" may represent such a dramatic and unsocialized change in the middle-aged mother's social world that she may be completely unprepared to cope with it. Pauline Bart (1968) has related the incidence of psychiatric disorder among middle-aged women to the physical and emotional leave-taking of children, for women whose social systems had been built around the role of mother.

These and other crises facing the aging individual are usually discussed under the general topic of "old age as a social problem" (see Loether, 1967; Atchley, 1972). In the present discussion, the thing to be noted is the prominent lack of institutional provisions—that is, the "outer" aspects of socialization—to assist the individual in adapting to the marked changes in the social system that are a usual concomitant to growing old. Irving Rosow has called this "the crowning insult to old age in our society." As the proportion and number of aged members of our population increase, so too will the need for more specific socialization mechanisms to assist the passage from one age status to another in late life (Rosow, 1967).

Summary: the social system and aging Section Two began with the notion of social time-clocks and the way in which expectations, rights, and duties are differentially distributed depending on how long one has occupied a particular position in a social institution. The social system of individuals is not static, but changes as they age and accept new positions and responsibilities throughout the life-cycle. Change can be seen in the roles, norms, statuses, and reference groups that constitute the basic dimensions of interpersonal behavior. Adaptation to such change over time in the social system is facilitated by socialization: both preparation by the social system and internalization by the individual, of the expectations and behaviors associated with a new social position.

A review was presented of findings concerning age grading, age norms, stereotypes, normlessness, and reference groups in adulthood and old age. There does seem to be a definite age-status system in our society which differentiates among appropriate and inappropriate behaviors on the basis of broad age classifications. However, there are very few norms regarding valuable or worthwhile behavior in old age. There are characteristic changes in role performance with advancing years; but little in the way of new roles open to an individual when he achieves "old age." There is little evidence that an elderly reference group exists to offer some patterning of behavioral expectancies. There is, in short, change, but little in the way of formal socialization to prepare the individual for the social changes normally associated with later life.

3   Aging and the Personal System

Our central theme is that the life course of individuals as they move through time is characterized by both continuity and change. That unfolding biography can best be viewed, I have suggested, in noting developmental events (as they occur in the biophysiological, social, and psychological domains) and in examining the consequences of those events in the adaptive mechanisms of behavior.

The resolution of this tension between continuity and change over time can perhaps best be seen in the *personal system:* the individual's unique and systematic organization of traits, motives, self-concept and style of life. In Section Two it was noted that the new social positions an individual occupies with the passage of time, and the norms attendant to these positions, become internalized through the process of socialization. It has been emphasized that the social system is not static and that the roles, norms, and reference groups which govern much of an individual's behavior change as he grows older and moves through successive age-related positions. What, then, about age-related change on the more personal or intrapsychic level of behavior? To what extent are there age-related shifts in personality organization, self-concept, and life-cycle associated with changes in the social system?

The principal underlying and unifying concept in this section is *adaptation:* how the individual continually makes adjustments to the changing conditions of his life as he grows older. Physiological changes in old age impose one set of conditions requiring adaptation; role and position changes impose another set. In summarizing the relatively short history of social-psychological research in aging, Havighurst has stressed the growing importance which the concept of an adaptational system has assumed:

> *This twenty-year series of studies has brought us to the conclusion that personality organization and coping style is the major factor in the life adjustment of the individual as he grows older. It is the manner in which the individual deals with the various contingencies in his life, some of them social, some biological, which is the important fact. It is what one makes of the world that is the important thing (Havighurst, 1968: 68).*

As we move from a discussion of the outer, or environmental, influences on behavior in old age, into a discussion of the inner, more unique aspects of behavior, we should again be reminded of the systematic wholeness of what we are describing and of the interplay between outer and inner states. This continuity over time has been aptly described thus:

> *In a sense the aging individual becomes a socio-emotional "institution" with the passage of time. Not only do certain personality processes provide continuity, but the individual has built up around him a network of social relationships which supports and maintains him. The "institutional" quality involves an individuated pattern of strategies for dealing with the changing world within and without, strategies which transcend many of the intra-psychic changes and (social) losses that appear (Neugarten, 1965b: 16).*

For purposes of description, the personal system may be divided into three parts corresponding to an implicit division of research endeavors in this area. The first part consists of personality variables such as traits, attitudes, motivational patterns, and mood tone. The second part is the self-concept (the reflection of the self upon the self) or a sense of identity. The third part is the style of life or activity patterns. Many writers have subsumed all these areas of investigation under the term *personality* (Birren, 1964; Chown, 1967), but there is good reason, especially in the field of aging, to be more precise by differentiating among the classes of variables just described.

PERSONALITY TRAITS OR MOTIVES AND AGING

Covert vs. overt personality processes There is much evidence concerning the continuity of personality and the stability of certain traits or underlying dispositions into old age. On the other hand, there are also indications of age-related *changes* in traits, motivational patterns, and what may be called ego energy, especially in old age.

Much of the information to be reviewed here comes from studies associated with the Kansas City Studies of Adult Life (Neugarten, 1968). In this research program a pool of over 700 individuals, built from probability samples of adults aged 40 to 90 who were living in their own homes, furnished a variety of data ranging from in-depth interviews to projective tests. A panel of 275 men and women furnished interviews over a six-year period. The investigators were particularly concerned with operationalizing constructs from the field of ego psychology. In one study, for example, Erikson's (1950) stages of ego development were explored. Another study described the personality types to be found among a sample group of aged individuals.

In these varied studies on dimensions of personality in middle and late life, two general findings emerged. On the one hand, change over time could be inferred in those "covert" personality processes not readily amenable to conscious control:

> In general, significant and consistent age differences emerged where projective data were used and where the investigator's attention was upon such issues as the perception of the self in relation to the external environment, or with ways of coping with impulse life. For example, in TAT data, 40-year-olds seemed to see themselves as possessing energy congruent with the opportunities presented in the outer world; while 60-year-olds seemed to see the environment as complex and dangerous, and to see the self as conforming and accommodating to outer world demands. This change was described in one of our studies as a movement from active to passive mastery (Neugarten, 1965b: 11).

Preoccupation with inner life, as opposed to persons and objects in the outer world, increased with advanced age groups. There was evidence of an increased saliency of inner life—what Neugarten calls "the increased interiority of personality" (Neugarten, 1969).

On the other hand, some personality dimensions did not seem affected by age-related change. These were the more "overt" aspects of personality related more closely to the social system:

On the other hand, age did not emerge as a significant source of variation when the investigator's attention was primarily upon socioadaptational patterns more than upon intrapsychic processes per se, and upon certain broadly-defined adaptive qualities of personality. Thus when the focus was upon generalized variables such as Erikson's "generativity" or "integrity," or upon "differentiated social perceptions" or "super-ego control," no age differences were found. Also in a typology based on factorial structures of personality, both middle-aged and older persons were to be found in each of the major types that emerged (Neugarten, 1965b: 12).

It seems, then, that there is one set of psychological processes which does reflect age differences. These are "intrapsychic" phenomena which are not readily available to awareness or conscious control and which do not have direct expression in overt patterns of social behavior. A second set of processes—relating more to personal-social adjustment or psychological well-being, as well as to typology of personality traits —do *not* seem to reflect age variation. Overt personality processes seem to change with age; covert processes reflect stability over time.

These findings are congruent with several other investigations in the field. Age-related shifts in covert personality dimensions have been reported by other investigators in terms of introversion, eccentricity, flattened affect, restriction of Rorschach responses, rigidity, cautiousness, and risk-taking (see Chown, 1967, for a review of these findings). Neugarten likens this to a "shrinkage of psychological life space" in old age (1965b:12). On the other hand, when the focus is on overt processes, other research supports the notion of stability in the more socioadaptive qualities of personality, such as life satisfaction (Neugarten, Havighurst, and Tobin, 1961), various tests of psychiatric and interpersonal functioning (Birren et al., 1963), or personality type (Reichard, Livson, and Petersen, 1962; Neugarten, Crotty, and Tobin, 1964). In this regard, Neugarten suggests that:

The implication is that other factors such as work status, health, financial resources, and marital status, are more cogent than chronological age in influencing degrees of adjustment in persons aged 50 and over (Neugarten, 1965b:13).

Personality typologies Are there definable types of aging personality? Reichard, Livson, and Petersen (1962) attempted to assess the personality characteristics of 87 men aged 55 to 84. Ratings on 115 personality variables were made on the basis of extensive open-ended interviews, some lasting 12 hours. Five patterns of personality types were described: (1) the mature—well-integrated persons who enjoyed whatever they were doing at the moment; (2) the rocking chair—passive-dependent men who were glad to take it easy when retirement came; (3) the armored—men whose motto was, "I've gotta keep active or I'll die" and who used this as a defense against age; (4) the angry—men who adjusted poorly to aging, who blamed others for their disappointments and lack of success; (5) the self-haters—depressed and gloomy, poorly adjusted to old age, who blamed themselves for frustrations and failures. Despite some methodological shortcomings, this study is an extremely interesting attempt to systematize global personal reactions to old age. A somewhat similar typology by Havinghurst, Neugarten, and Tobin will be discussed later in terms of "patterns of aging."

AGING AND SELF-CONCEPT

The term "self-concept" is extremely important in the study of personal organization. It refers to *the attitude and evaluation an individual has concerning himself* or, to use a traditional sociological formulation, the way the "self as object" is evaluated (Mead, 1934). It is similar to Erikson's concept of "identity" as something which is never gained nor maintained once and for all and thus is quite open to change and development over time (Gordon, forthcoming).

Our self-concept is highly interrelated with other people's perceptions of us. It is useful to think of it as the impression a man makes on others and the impression he makes on himself (Chown, 1967). In this same respect, Erikson suggests identity is the creation of a sense of sameness between the personality felt by the individual and that recognized by others, a sense of consistency with one's past self and the future (Erikson, 1950).

Self-concept is thus a higher order of abstraction than the specific personality traits and patterns just discussed. It refers to the process and product of the "self reflecting on itself" and has both a different scope and a different flavor from such trait descriptions as say, aggressiveness or introversion of authoritarianism.

I think it is useful to think of a person's attitudes toward himself as having three aspects. The *cognitive* component represents the content of the self—"I am intelligent, useful, sincere, ambitious." The *affective* component reflects one's feelings about oneself—"I am satisfied with the way I act; I don't like my prominent nose; I wish I were more outgoing." The *behavioral* component is the tendency to act toward oneself in various ways: a person may behave as if he has a high regard for himself; he may be self-effacing and deprecatory, like Dicken's Uriah Heep; or he may show oversensitivity to certain of his characteristics, like Herblock's cartoons of the presidents.

How and why does the self-concept change over time? One of the most promising formulations of both stability and change in adult personality focuses on the interrelationship between self-concept and the behavior of others (Secord and Backman, 1961). This model describes the organization of behavior in terms of relations among three components: an individual's self-concept *(S)*, his interpretation of behavior *(B)*, and the behavior of others in relation to him *(O)*. The central notion of the model is that individuals act in order to maintain a state of congruity among the three. Congruity exists when *B* and *O* imply a definition of the individual that is congruent with *S*—as, for example, when a young woman thinks she is attractive, acts in a way that she interprets as pleasing, and is made to feel that others respond to her as an attractive person. Incongruity between *S*, *B*, and *O*, on the other hand, gives rise to disruptions in stability and calls for a reorganization of the self. Such incongruities can be ignored (denial), they can overwhelm the individual so that he revives older modes of response (regression), or they can be accepted and adequately met (adaptation and/or continued development).

Here we begin to see the interplay between the social and personal systems with aging. The changing roles and related behaviors of different "punctuation points" of the adult life-cycle, such as retirement, old age, or widowhood, can be viewed as disruptions in the previous balance of *S-B-O* requiring a reorganization of the self. In each case, the conception an individual has of himself must be altered in view of changes in the way the social system treats him (*O*) and changes in his own pattern of customary behavior (*B*) (see Bortner, 1967; Gordon, 1973).

There is reason to believe that age brings changes in the self-concept as the result of changes in the social system. One principal contributor to the self-concept is the *roles* which an individual plays and the way in which he plays them (McCall and Simmons, 1966). To the extent that these roles are sequential and discontinuous, with movement from one to the next requiring certain behavior changes (as when a man passes from bachelor to father to grandfather), they are instrumental in bringing about certain changes in the self. They cause, in short, a transformation of identity (Strauss, 1969). For example, in old age a new and less valued self-image may be thrust upon an individual whose major source of identity has been associated with occupational roles. As described by Cavan:

> At the point of compulsory retirement . . . the means of carrying out the social role disappears: the man is a lawyer without a case, a bookkeeper without books, a machinist without tools. Second, he is excluded from his group of former co-workers: as an isolated person he may be completely unable to function in his former role. Third, as a retired person, he begins to find a different evaluation of himself in the minds of others from the evaluation he had as an employed person. He no longer sees respect in the eyes of former subordinates, praise in the faces of former superiors, and approval in the manner of former co-workers. The looking glass composed of his former important groups throws back a changed image: he is done for, an old-timer, old-fashioned, on the shelf (Cavan, 1962: 527-528).

LIFE STYLE AND AGING

The third dimension of the personal system to be considered here is the most general, and also the most explicitly related to continuity over time in the personal system. Life style has not been greatly used in the analysis of individual behavior, perhaps because of the global nature of the concept and the associated difficulty in operationalization. Life style can be defined as *the observable organization of an individual's activities in terms of his use of time, his investment of energy, and his choice of interpersonal objects.* This concept provides another useful bridge between the personal and the social systems in analyzing what occurs over the life-cycle (Maddox, 1970).

The available research in this area points to considerable continuity over time in life style. In the most extensive study to date in this area, Williams and Wirths (1965) carried out exhaustive case studies of 168 elderly respondents from the Kansas City Studies of Adult Life, all of whom had been interviewed seven times in a five-and-one-half year period. They delineated six "styles of life" which seemed to characterize the "action system" of individuals over that time period. Their goal was to relate these styles of life to a definition of successful aging. The six styles which emerge from their analysis and the percentage of individuals from the sample of 168 who could be placed in each category are as follows: (1) World of work (15 percent); (2) Familism (33 percent); (3) Living alone (13 percent); (4) Couplehood (20 percent); (5) Easing through life with minimal involvement (7 percent); (6) Living fully (13 percent). What is the relation between these styles and their global measure of "successful aging"? Interestingly enough, they found very successful and very unsuccessful aging in each category, though the styles of "Familism" and "Living fully" had a higher percentage of successful individuals than did the other. They note that "each style presents its own special problems which must be met to age successfully, and its own supports which favor success" (Williams and Wirths, 1965: 200).

PATTERNS OF AGING

Recent work by Havighurst, Neugarten, and Tobin (1968) represents perhaps the most promising attempt to integrate variables in the personal and social systems as they relate to the global adaptation of individuals to aging. In their formulation, based on data from the Kansas City Studies, they describe life styles in later maturity as *patterns of aging:*

> *A pattern of aging is a coherent complex of behavior, including social interaction and use of free time, achieved by an individual through the interaction of his personality with his physical organism and with his social setting. There is a limited number of patterns which can be discovered empirically. (Havighurst, 1968: 71).*

Three kinds of data are used in this description: (1) personality type, as established by factor analysis of 45 personality variables; (2) extent of social role activity; and (3) degree of life satisfaction or psychological well-being manifest by the individuals being studied. In combining these three sets of measures, they describe eight patterns of aging in their 70-79 age group. These are indicated in Table 2. They call their first pattern the "re-organizers," individuals who were characterized by high role activity,

Table 2. Personality type in relation to role activity and life satisfaction (age 70-79) in the Kansas City study

Personality type	Role activity	Life Satisfaction* High	Medium	Low
Integrated	High	(9) A	2	
	Medium	(5) B		
	Low	(3) C		
Armored-defended	High	(5) D		
	Medium	6	1 ⎫ E	
	Low	(2)	1 ⎭	1
Passive-dependent	High		1 ⎫ F	
	Medium	(1)	4 ⎭	
	Low	2	(3)	(2) G
Unintegrated	High		2	1
	Medium	1		
	Low		(2)	(5) H
	Total	34	16	9

PATTERNS OF AGING

A: Reorganizer   C: Disengaged   E: Constricted   G: Apathetic
B: Focused   D: Holding on   F: Succorance Seeker   H: Disorganized

*The numbers refer to the number of individuals. Those which are circled singly or grouped together represent the eight patterns of aging (A-H).

(N = 59)

Source: Neugarten, 1965a: 253.

satisfaction, and a personality type termed "integrated." The second pattern, the "focused," included individuals who were also high in life-satisfaction and of the integrated category of personality; their social role activity level was medium. A third pattern, the "holding on," were high in life satisfaction, high to medium in role activity level, and of the "armored-defended" personality type. To give one final example, the "disorganized" pattern of aging was applied to those individuals low in role activity level, medium to low in life satisfaction, and of the "unintegrated" personality type. The remaining four patterns occurred less frequently, as illustrated in Table 2.

Neugarten has aptly summarized the results of this attempt to systematize interrelations between the personal and the social systems when looking at the process of aging:

... we regard personality as the pivotal dimension in describing patterns of aging and in predicting relationships between level of social role activity and life satisfaction. There is considerable evidence that, in normal men and women, there is no sharp discontinuity of personality with age, but instead an increasing consistency. Those characteristics that have been central to the personality seem to become even more clearly delineated, and those values the individual has been cherishing become even more salient. In the personality that remains integrated—and in an environment that permits—patterns of overt behavior are likely to become increasingly consonant with the individual's underlying personality needs and his desires (Neugarten, 1965a: 254).

The interpenetration of social interaction patterns and psychological processes in old age is perhaps most dramatically indicated in analyses of aging and mental disorder. Professor Marjorie Lowenthal and her associates have focused on social processes in aging and adaptation in a series of studies spanning two decades (see Lowenthal, Berkmann, and associates, 1967). One of the more dramatic findings in this program of research concerns the importance of a confidant in old age (Lowenthal and Haven, 1968). That is, maintenance of a long-term, intimate relationship is more closely associated with good mental health than is high social interaction or high status; losses such as widowhood or retirement are ameliorated by the presence of a confidant. Thus, from this perspective the crucial variable in the analysis of social system correlates of psychological well-being is the presence or absence of a confidant—not high or low role activity or high social status per se. A second important finding in this research concerns continuity in patterns of intimacy or isolation which people carry with them into old age. Lowenthal found many instances of solitary older people living in the community. For these, isolation was a life-long pattern and was not related to psychiatric impairment.

Summary: the personal system and adaptation to aging The process of adaptation in the developing biographies of individuals can be seen in the ways they react to the physiological and social changes—often decremental in character—that occur with aging. There is both continuity and change in the personal system as individuals adapt to developmental events involving role change and decreased saliency of norms in later maturity.

From the standpoint of personality traits and motives, there is evidence of change in the more covert intrapsychic processes: a greater degree of introversion, an increased saliency of inner life, a withdrawal of energy from external events and social objects. On the other hand there is evidence of stability in overt, socioadaptational processes. Such dimensions as interpersonal functioning, psychological well-being, and general life style are less prone to change with the passage of time. Changes of the body and social system require a reorganization of the self-concept;

under successful conditions this involves an acceptance of the status of being aged and restructuring one's life around decreasing energy and body resources. The various adaptational profiles in aging can best be seen in terms of life style or patterns of aging—the global pattern of expenditures of time and energy as individuals respond to the constraints and opportunities provided by the social system.

4 Theories of Aging: Scientific and Applied

We have seen that with the passage of time the behavior of individuals as they age is the product of continuous interplay between elements of the social system and of the personal system. We have seen that aging is a process of both continuity and change: change in that the developing individual experiences a variety of developmental events with the passage of time; continuity in that he responds to these events from the resources of his own history of adaptation.

I want to turn now from a focus on conceptual frameworks and data relevant to the sociology of age, to more general considerations about theory, implications, and application of this knowledge. At some point every scientist, in the midst of his data gathering and statistical manipulations, is brought up short by a question such as the following: "That's all very nice, but what does it *mean*? Of what *practical use* is your work?" Such embarrassing questions are often put to him by practitioners whose careers demand the application of the best of knowledge to the betterment of others. Some readers of this essay, for instance, may be public administrators in the field of aging or students in the helping professions, such as medicine, social work, or occupational therapy. A sociological view of aging touches directly their concerns. But at this point they might justifiably ask, "What is the outcome of all the research reviewed on the personal and social system in old age? How are these findings relevant to the question of how to structure a nursing home, or a walk-in Senior Citizens center?"

What the public and practitioners demand of scientists at some point is a concise, jargon-free statement of findings that at least summarize the investigations in his field and at best make clear policy implications. When faced with such demands most social scientists—myself included—are inclined to demur, pointing out that: (a) we do not yet possess adequate scientific knowledge to make such practical interventions with a high degree of predictability of outcome; (b) the making of public policy is not the office of scientists; we will work in our laboratories, doing our scientific work well, and let other professionals apply our findings. However, such aloofness from the world of everyday affairs is not desirable from the standpoint of either scientific objectivity or humanitarian concern, for one criteria in judging the adequacy of a sociological theory is its pragmatic utility (see Lemon, Bengtson, and Peterson, 1972).

Furthermore, there is the issue of the social responsibility of the scientists. Like it or not, social scientists are increasingly faced with the demand to present their findings in a tight package from which practical applications may be correctly deduced. This means the development of theory that has both logical (scientific) and pragmatic utility.

THE CURRENT STATE OF THEORY IN SOCIAL GERONTOLOGY

The function of theory in social science is to integrate current knowledge, to explain empirically based findings, and to predict new relationships. Theory is used for both the scientist and the practitioner in a field like gerontology, for it both organizes observation and suggests policy implementation (Atchley, 1972). A social theory of aging, if it is to meet the demands of the scientific community at least, should first of all integrate such findings as reported in this monograph; second, it should offer a cogent system of explanation for the various phenomena that have been reviewed; third, it should predict the future: "if this, and this, and this occurs; then that will surely follow."

Is there theory in social gerontology that fits these criteria? Not at the present time. Indeed, it is unlikely that we will have in the foreseeable future such grand theory that ties together the complex phenomena in the social and personal systems as they change through time. Effort is probably better spent in developing what Merton has called "theories in the middle range." Even in this relatively modest attempt at theory building, there are several difficulties which have hindered progress.

First, there is the lack of an adequately large and scientifically sound body of facts concerning social and psychological processes in aging. Scientific theory is based on facts—facts produced in the course of scientific investigation which are both objective (reliable) and valid. But in the everyday world of personal and social behavior, where the sociologist most often makes his observations, the data are necessarily more crude, more subject to fluctuation and unmeasured influences, less reliable and objective, than those produced in the natural scientist's laboratory. Even the most careful social investigators very often suspect that their results would be quite different if they had a slightly different sample, worded their questions slightly differently, or even employed a different frame of reference in approaching the problem.

Second, social research is extremely expensive and time consuming. A generation of humans ages and changes more slowly than a cohort of rats. In terms of the personality changes discussed earlier, for example, we must wait a long time to see the manifestation of continuity or change over time.

And finally, remember that the field of aging is a relatively young scientific area. The first book that may be termed a social-psychological investigation of aging appeared in 1953 (Havighurst and Albrecht); the first collection of comprehensive research review papers regarding sociological aspects of aging appeared in 1960 (Tibbitts). For these reasons, therefore—the difficulty in getting scientific facts, the expense of research, and the short history of the field—there is no theory at present that interrelates adequately the phenomena reviewed in the first two parts of this section.

There have been attempts, however; and a great deal of research in the field has been stimulated by attempts to tie together the multifaceted phenomena of aging under the rubric of "disengagement" or "activity" theories of aging. Though these are hardly theories in the strict sense of the word, they perform much of the function of theory by systematizing some of the information about aging and making certain predictions about behavior in old age.

ACTIVITY THEORY OF AGING

The first orientation may be called the activity theory of aging. This is the "common sense" or lay theory of aging, since it reflects the expectations most often reflected in newspaper columns, "Golden Age" magazines, and even legislative programs directed to old age. Recall that Johann Johnson, the 73-year-old grandfather, said that his only real goal was to "keep active—I want to wear out, not rust out."

As reflected in the earliest social-psychological survey of aging, this orientation can be characterized as follows:

> The American formula for happiness in old age might be summed up in the phrase "keep active." ... Concluding from this public opinion study we should say that the American society desires and expects a good deal of activity and independence from its older people ... We want them to be fairly active. We do not want them to isolate themselves and merely vegetate. (Havighurst and Albrecht, 1953: 55, 37, 47)

To put all this more precisely in the framework outlined in this essay: activity theory suggests that the relationship between the social system and the personal system remains fairly stable as an individual passes from the status of middle age into the status of old age. The norms impinging upon him do not markedly change; he is still expected to do much the same as he did in the middle years, with the exception that he is allowed not to work (whether he wants to or not) and he is expected to "slow down a little" (Havighurst and Albrecht, 1953: 37). When roles are taken from him, as occurs with retirement or with the loss of friends or spouse, he is expected to compensate by increasing activity in other spheres or with other people. The sources of satisfaction, his self-concept, and life style, are not expected to change much from what they were in the middle years. In America, it appears there is an expectation that the broader society is to meet these continuing needs for activity by structuring certain aspects of the environment (such as Golden Age centers, and nursing homes) to encourage interaction more than privacy. However, other conditions relevant to the needs of elderly individuals are pretty much ignored (such as transportation systems enabling the urban aged to be really mobile, or the location of hospitals and health centers in the economically most feasible areas rather than where great numbers of aged live). In short, despite some changes in the social system, the activity theory of aging emphasizes the stability of personal system orientations as individuals grow older, and deemphasizes the need for social-structural alterations of any significant magnitude. In activity theory one can see the ethic of rugged American individualism at work (Kuypers and Bengtson, 1973).

The activity orientation to aging has remained more a set of assumptions about social-psychological processes in aging than an explicit and testable theory. However, one attempt has been made to systematically state the major propositions and relationships of the theory, and then test it with data. Lemon, Bengtson, and Peterson (1972) isolated what appeared to be two central propositions of activity theory. The first is that there is a positive relationship between social activity and life satisfaction in old age (because the role support inherent in social activity is related to a positive self concept). The second proposition is that salient role loss (such as widowhood and retirement) is inversely related to life satisfaction. The data (from a sample of older people moving into a retirement community) did *not* support these propositions. Only social activity with friends was in any way related to life satisfaction. In short, this study raises some serious questions regarding the adequacy of "activity theory" of aging. It does not seem that the maintenance of high activity levels is invariably related to "successful aging," despite our tendency to assume this in planning programs for the elderly.

DISENGAGEMENT THEORY

A very different perspective is presented by the disengagement theory of aging (Cumming and Henry, 1961). Here the aging process is seen as a mutual, and inevitable, *"disengaging"* of the individual and society. The individual gradually withdraws socially as well as psychologically from his environment as he moves into old age. Most importantly, the process of withdrawal is suggested by the theory to be mutually satisfying. For the individual, this withdrawal brings a release from the societal pressures for instrumental performance that tax a weakening body. For the society, this withdrawal allows younger (and, presumably, more energetic and competent) individuals to assume the functional roles which must be fulfilled for the survival of the social system. This is, of course, an example of "sociological functionalism."

Cumming and Henry presented data to indicate that there is a measurable decrease in the individual's psychological engagement, or ego-involvement, in the external environment. They interpreted their data to mean that associated with this generally lower level of social engagement and ego-involvement in the external world, there is a *high* level of psychological well-being, or, as they defined it, "morale."

Placed within the framework of this book, the central contribution of disengagement theory is its attempt to interrelate physiological, psychological, and social changes in old age. Furthermore, this theory emphasizes the disjunctive, developmental quality of passage into old age. It suggests that old age *is* different from middle age, marked by substantial shifts—and eventually a new equilibrium of forces—in the social and personal systems. The sources of psychological well-being in old age, for example, are much different than those in middle age, when they were much more dependent on continued and face-to-face interaction with others in the social environment. Similarly, there is a difference in the extent to which social norms impinge on the individual and are the immediate causes of his behavior: expectations are much less salient. In short, the theory points to a change in balance between the social and the personal systems.

Disengagement theory, then, in contrast to activity theory, is a specific attempt to integrate findings concerning social-psychological phenomena in old age, to explain successful aging, and to state some of the conditions associated with happiness in old age. How has this theory fared in the subsequent research which it has inspired?

In the past few years, disengagement theory has become a focal point for discussion and research about the aging process (see Rose, 1964; Maddox, 1970; Atchley, 1972). Though it is generally accepted that there is a decrease in overall social activity with age (Havighurst, Neugarten, and Tobin, 1968; Maddox, 1963), there has been considerable disagreement with the proposition that this social disengagement is an inevitable or universal process and that there is an inverse relationship in old age between activity and life satisfaction (Tobin and Neugarten, 1961; Maddox, 1963; Palmore, 1968).

For example, Kutner (1962) suggests that there is a "re-integration and re-differentiation" of activity in social roles, rather than a near universal decrease, with old age. By extension, it can be argued that social, not biological, factors are most prominent in this process. That is, the constraints imposed by developmental events in the social system, and the personal system's response to those changes, determine disengagement —not physiological or exclusively intrapsychic factors. In presenting data from a longitudinal study, Maddox (1963) concludes that there is a significant *positive* relationship between activity and "morale" rather than the reverse, as implied by disengagement theory. Indeed, in subsequent analyses of data from the Kansas City Study of Adult life, colleagues of Cumming and Henry have suggested that the modal pattern seems to be more "high engagement and high satisfaction" than "low engagement and high satisfaction" (Havighurst, Neugarten, and Tobin, 1968). This pattern was also found in the cross-national study of retirement (see Bengtson, Chiriboga, and Keller, 1969).

Perhaps the most clear indication of the limitations of both activity and disengagement theories of aging comes from the work of Havighurst and Neugarten on patterns of aging (refer to Table 2). Here it is clear that neither model accounts for the empirical relationship of social activity, personality types, and psychological well-being. As summarized by Neugarten:

> People, as they grow old, seem to be neither at the mercy of the social environment nor at the mercy of some set of intrinsic processes—in either instance, inexorable changes that they cannot influence. On the contrary, the individual seems to continue to make his own "impress" upon the wide range of social and biological changes. He continues to exercise choice and to select from the environment in accordance with his own long-established needs. He ages according to a pattern that has a long history, and that maintains itself, with adaptation, to the end of life (Neugarten, 1965a: 254).

THE SOCIAL RECONSTRUCTION MODEL

From the evidence presented in this paper, it seems clear that new social-psychological models of aging is needed. Such models must take into account the systems of variables outlined at the beginning of this monograph: developmental and historical events as they impinge on the social and personal systems in individual behavior. It may be premature at present for such an attempt to be made, since concepts and variables in these systems are less well-defined than one would like, and we are only beginning to have the benefit of replicated findings in many of these areas. The next decade, however, promises to be an extremely exciting one in the sociology of aging as current studies add to information about these systems and the impact of these events. In concluding this chapter, it seems useful to sketch out what these new approaches to theory in the sociology and social psychology of aging will probably be like.

Emergent perspectives in theory building   First, it is likely that future social research in gerontology will pursue research that is less exploratory, more limited, and more guided by explicit theory derived from other areas of investigation, than in the past. At the same time, the concern will probably remain fixed on the general interrelations between the social system, broadly conceived, and the personal system. More baseline data will be gathered to fill out the leads presented by the Prairie City and Kansas City researchers: the existence and perception of norms regarding behavior in old age; the correlates of these norms and their variation by social class, sex, culture, and role system; how such elements of the social system impinge on the individual, and with what effect on self-concept, life satisfaction, and life style.

Second, it is likely that future research will be even more practice oriented than in previous decades. Funding agencies (such as the National Institutes of Mental Health) are under increasing pressure to demonstrate the immediate and practical relevance of the research they support. Therefore more funds are likely to be allocated to demonstration projects and less to "basic" research. This means researchers will have to be even more careful to spell out the potential applications of their efforts.

Third, I think that research traditions and theories from the mainstream of sociology and social psychology will more frequently be applied to the problem of change over time. Some of these, such as Secord and Backman's (1961) model of personality stability or change, only await application in research. Others, such as Festinger's dissonance-choice orientation or the exchange model of Thibaut and Kelley (see Jones and Gerard, 1967, for excellent reviews of both traditions) could be profitably modified and applied to such problems as retirement transition and the maintenance of positive self-image in retirement.

Still other theoretical orientations, such as the interactionist and structural-functional perspectives in sociology, have already been applied willy-nilly to certain problems in the field (activity and disengagement theories respectively correspond to these traditions). However, researchers interested in aging should systematically explore the insights of these perspectives as they apply to issues in the life cycle.

Finally, a most promising application of stratification theory in sociology has recently been presented by Riley, Johnson, and Foner (1972). The perspective of age stratification promises to generate many useful propositions and data regarding age as a dimension of social organization in the next few years.

The "Social Reconstruction Syndrome" In concluding this section, let us look at one example of a new theoretical perspective which borrows from several theoretical traditions in attempting to characterize positive or negative processes in aging. The principal intellectual roots of this perspective are in "labeling theory" in community psychiatry, which is related to the symbolic interactionist tradition in sociology. The "Social Reconstruction Syndrome" (Kuypers and Bengtson, 1973) represents an example of wedding labeling theory to components of systems theory and applying them to practical problems of adjustment in aging—seen at both the macro- and micro-levels of social context.

It has long been asserted that mental health and illness are quite directly related to social-environmental conditions. As has been emphasized through this book, our self-concept depends in part on the way we perform in our everyday social positions and the way others react to us. The concept of a "Social Breakdown Syndrome" has been presented by Zusman (1966) to characterize the process by which a person's social environment can interact with his self-concept to produce a vicious spiral of negative psychological functioning. Zussman proposes a seven-stage cycle of "Social Breakdown" in which the most important steps are (1) the organism's precondition of susceptibility to psychological breakdown (having problem with identity or inappropriate standards concerning social relationships); (2) the labeling of the individual by those around him as incompetent or deficient in some respect; (3) his induction into a sick, dependent role, learning the behavior associated with that role and the atrophy of previous skills; (4) the individual's identification with the "sick" role and self-identification as inadequate. Then the malignant cycle begins again, for the individual is even more susceptible to subsequent steps in psychological breakdown (see Figure 1).

Figure 1. THE SOCIAL BREAKDOWN SYNDROME: A vicious cycle of increasing incompetence

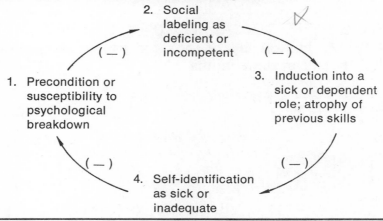

Kuypers and I suggested that the Social Breakdown Syndrome could be applied in examining the problems of aging in contemporary American society. The Social Breakdown orientation suggests that an individual's sense of self, his ability to mediate between self and society, and his orientation to competence are related to the kinds of social labeling and valuing he experiences in aging. In terms of the first stage of social breakdown, we argued that the elderly are likely to be susceptible to and dependent on social labeling because of the nature of social reorganization in later life. That is, role loss, vague or inappropriate normative information, and lack of reference groups all serve to deprive the individual of feedback concerning who he is, what roles and behaviors he can perform, and what value he is to his social world. Second, this feedback vacuum creates a vulnerability to, and dependence on, external sources of self-labeling, many of which communicate a stereotypic portrayal of the elderly as useless and obsolete—a characterization common in a society which places so much importance on productivity. Third, the individual who accepts such negative labeling is then inducted into the negative, dependent position—learning to act like old people are supposed to act—and previous skills of independence atrophy. Fourth, he accepts the external labeling and identifies himself as inadequate, setting the stage for another vicious spiral. Thus, the Social Breakdown Syndrome characterizes the dynamic relationship between susceptibility, negative labeling, and the development of psychological weakness. We have suggested it applies to many elderly individuals in American Society.

In a cyclical system one can structure inputs at many levels; how might the vicious cycle of Social Breakdown be broken? The efforts of practitioners and planners to meet needs of an aging population represent attempts to make beneficial inputs to this end. We suggested that the process be viewed as a "Social Reconstruction Syndrome." This model (see Figure 2) does two things: (1) it characterizes the dynamic interaction between the individual and his social system as he moves through

Figure 2. THE SOCIAL RECONSTRUCTION SYN-DROME: A benign cycle of increasing competence through social system inputs

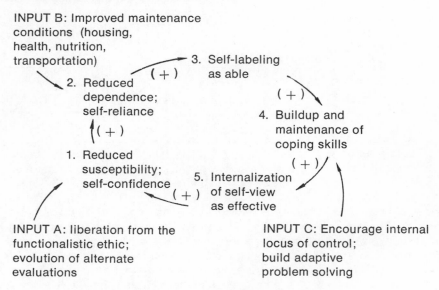

INPUT B: Improved maintenance conditions (housing, health, nutrition, transportation)

2. Reduced dependence; self-reliance

(+)

3. Self-labeling as able

(+)

4. Buildup and maintenance of coping skills

(+)

1. Reduced susceptibility; self-confidence

5. Internalization of self-view as effective

(+)

INPUT A: liberation from the functionalistic ethic; evolution of alternate evaluations

INPUT C: Encourage internal locus of control; build adaptive problem solving time, and (2) it portrays some inputs which can be made to assist the elderly.

Entries outside the circle (i.e., external inputs to the system) are conditions of the environment and activities of practitioners which aid the establishment of the Social Reconstruction Syndrome. The aged *are* vulnerable in our society—the latter stages of the life cycle imply many potential problems. Three major types of inputs to ameliorate these problems were suggested. First, efforts can be made to liberate the individual from an age-inappropriate view of status: the functional ethic, which suggests self-worth is contingent on performance in economic or "productive" social positions, is particularly inappropriate in old age. In counseling, for example, one might urge the older person to adopt a more "humanitarian" frame of self-judgment. A second type of input to the system affecting elderly individuals is improving social services to them or, to put it differently, enhancing adaptive capacity by lessening the debilitating environmental conditions faced by most older people, such as poor housing, poor health, and poverty. This would facilitate coping skills. Third, we suggested that, to enable the development of an internal locus of control, those who envision themselves as serving the elderly must divest some of their own power and control: self-determination by the elderly and individual control of policy and administration is the foundation for competent aging.

Imagine, for example, an old age home whose personal and decision-making bodies are exclusively comprised of the elderly themselves. While the nursing and social service staff, for example, might be younger people, they are servants of the elderly board of directors, the elderly committee structure, and the elderly administrators. Imagine a program of continuing education entirely defined and run by the elderly, supported by society and government, but in no way controlled by the extension division of existing colleges and universities. This would enhance the internal control which is the hallmark of competence.

The Social Reconstruction model characterizing aging invites the alteration of the system by intervention at any point. Input can be made by practitioners (interested in helping the aging individual) or by the political order (concerned with the welfare of an aging population). A benign circle, rather than a vicious one, may be created; the question is how best to create inputs which will result in a positive reversal of the Social Breakdown Syndrome.

5 Summary

This book has focused on time, change, and everyday human behavior. The social scientist is concerned with individual behavior as it is influenced by social stimuli, as well as with the regularities of social interaction in sets of people. The sociologist interested in the life cycle, and in behavioral processes in aging and middle age, must begin by recognizing change with the passage of time in these behavioral processes— change in the social system and change in the personal system as individuals move through time. He must also recognize the considerable stability or continuity over time in these systems of behavior.

The social system may be conceptualized as a complex of roles, norms, status, and reference groups. As individuals become older, this complex changes over time. It is helpful to consider social as well as chronological definitions of age. Social age is the way in which expectations, rights, and rewards are distributed depending upon how long a person has occupied a particular position. The concept of socialization is important in understanding the mechanisms by which the society brings about changes in roles and norms, and the resulting internalization of these changes by the individual. Various age grades have been identified, although the accompanying norms may not always be explicit, particularly those relating especially to old age.

Both change and stability are also found in the personality or personal system of the individual over time. Many of the personality traits, especially the more overt aspects, appear to become institutionalized over time and to change little. However, more covert aspects of the personality do appear to change over time, with the aging person becoming more withdrawn from the external world and becoming more introspective. Some changes in the self-concept have also been identified which, in relation to successful aging, indicate the necessity of the acceptance of the status of being aged. Research has also shown continuity over time in life style or pattern of resource allocation, as well as the relationship of the various life styles to successful aging.

Because of the relative paucity of scientific data, attempts to build comprehensive social-psychological theories of aging may be premature at this time. However, three major theories have been identified. The activity theory emphasizes that successful aging consists in maintaining the former life and activities as long as possible and finds little change in either the personal or the social system with aging. Or, if there are changes, both the society and the person are expected to compensate for them. The disengagement theory emphasizes almost the opposite. In this view, successful aging involves the mutual withdrawal of both society and the individual from each other. The process is seen as functional for the individual because of his decreasing capacities and for society because it insures its own continuity by replacing the aging individual with a younger person. The social reconstruction theory sees adjustment to aging as a dynamic, precarious process of interaction between the individual and his social environment. It can be a vicious cycle (as in the Social Breakdown Syndrome) or it can be a benign one (seen as a spiral of personal mastery and positive social recognition). Inputs to the system come from practitioners (interested in the aging individual) and the political order (concerned with the welfare of the aged population). Hopefully such inputs will result in a Social Reconstruction Syndrome.

References

Atchley, R. A.
1972   The Social Forces in Later Life: An Introduction to Social Gerontology. Belmont, Calif. Wadsworth.

Bart, P.
1968   "Social structure and vocabularies of discomfort: what happened to female hysteria?" Journal of Health and Social Behavior 9:188-193.

Bengtson, V. L.
1969   "Cultural and occupational differences in level of present role activity in retirement." In Adjustment to Retirement: A Cross-National Study, ed. R. J. Havighurst, M. Thomae, B. L. Neugarten, and J. K. A. Munnichs. Assen, The Netherlands: Van Gorkum.
1970   "The generation gap: a review and typology of social-psychological perspectives." Youth and Society 2:7-32.
1971   "Inter-age perceptions and the generation gap." Gerontologist 11,4 (Part 2):85-89.

Bengtson, V. L. and K. D. Black
1973   "Inter-generational relations and continuities in socialization." In Life-Span Developmental Psychology: Personality and Socialization, ed. P. Baltes and W. Schaie. New York: Academic Press (forthcoming).

Bengtson, V. L., D. C. Chriboga, and A. C. Keller
1969   "Occupational differences in retirement: patterns of role activity and life-outlook among Chicago retired teachers and steelworkers." In Adjustment to Retirement: A Cross-National Study, ed. R. J. Havighurst, M. Thomae, B. L. Neugarten, and J. K. A. Munnichs. Assen, The Netherlands: Van Gorkum.

Birren, J. E.
1964   The Psychology of Aging. Englewood Cliffs, N. J.: Prentice-Hall.

Birren, J. E., R. N. Butler, S. W. Greenhouse, L. Sokoloff, and M. R. Yarrow, eds.
1963   Human Aging: A Biological and Behavioral Study. Bethesda, Md.: Public Health Service, Publication No. 986.

Bortner, R.
1967   "Personality and social psychology in the study of aging." Gerontologist 7, 2:23-36.

Brim, O., Jr.
1966   "Socialization after childhood." In Socialization through the Life Cycle by O. Brim, Jr. and S. Wheeler. New York: John Wiley.

Cain, L. E., Jr.
1964   "Life course and social structure." In Handbook of Modern Sociology, ed. R. E. L. Faris. Chicago: Rand McNally.

Cavan, R.
1962   "Self and role in adjustment during old age." In Human Behavior and Social Processes: An Interactionist Approach, ed. A. M. Rose. Boston: Houghton Mifflin.

Chown, S. M.
1967   "Personality and aging." Paper prepared for Conference on Theory and Research in Aging, Univ. of West Virginia, May 14.

Clark, M.
1967   "The anthropology of aging: a new area for studies of culture and personality." Gerontologist 7, 1:55-64.

Cumming, E. and W. Henry
1961   Growing Old. New York: Basic Books.

Cutler, N.
1970   "Generation, maturation, and party affiliation: a cohort analysis." Public Opinion Quarterly 33:583-588.

Deutscher, I.
1964   "The quality of postparental life: definition of the situation." Journal of Marriage and Family 26:52-59.

Erikson, E.
1950   Childhood and Society. New York: Norton.

Glick, P. C., D. M. Heer, and J. C. Beresford
1959   "Family formation and family composition: trends and prospects." Paper presented at the annual meeting of the American Association for the Advancement of Science, Chicago, December.

Goffman, E.
1966   Interaction Ritual. Garden City, N. Y.: Anchor.

Gordon, C.
1973   On Self Conceptions Development. Indianapolis: Bobbs-Merrill (forthcoming).

Havighurst, R. J.
1968   "A socio-psychological perspective of aging." Gerontologist 8:67-71.

Havighurst, R. J. and R. Albrecht
1953   Older People. New York: Longmans, Green.

Havighurst, R. J., B. L. Neugarten, and S. S. Tobin
1968   "Disengagement and patterns of aging." In Middle Age and Aging, ed. B. L. Neugarten. Chicago: Univ. of Chicago Press.

Havighurst, R. J., J. K. A. Munnichs, B. L. Neugarten, and M. Thomae, eds.
1969   Adjustment to Retirement: A Cross-National Study. Assen, The Netherlands: Van Gorkum.

Hickey, T. and R. A. Kalish
1968   "Young people's perception of adults." Journal of Gerontology 23:215-219.

Jones, E. B. and H. R. Gerard
1967   Foundations of Social Psychology. New York: John Wiley.

Kutner, B.
1962   "The social nature of aging." Gerontologist 2, 1:5-9.

Kuypers, J. A. and V. L. Bengtson
1973   "Competence and social breakdown: a social-psychological view of aging." Human Development 16, 2:37-49.

Lemon, B. W., V. L. Bengtson, and J. A. Peterson
1972   "Activity types and life satisfaction in a retirement community." Journal of Gerontology 27, 4:511-523.

Linton, R.
1940   "A neglected aspect of social organization." American Journal of Sociology 45:870-886.

Loether, H. J.
1967 Problems of Aging. Belmont, Calif.: Dickenson.

Lowenthal, M. F., P. L. Berkmann, and Associates
1967 Aging and Mental Disorder in San Francisco: A Social Psychiatric Study. San Francisco: Jossey-Bass.

Lowenthal, M. F. and C. Haven
1968 "Interaction and adaptation: intimacy as a critical variable." American Sociological Review 33.

Maddox, G.
1963 "Activity and morale: A longitudinal study of selected elderly subjects." Social Forces 42:195-204.
1966 "Retirement as a social event in the United States." In Aging and Social Policy, ed. J. C. McKinney and F. T. deVyver. New York: Appleton-Century-Crofts.
1970 "Persistence of life style among the elderly." In Normal Aging, ed. E. Palmore. Durham, N. C.: Duke Univ. Press.

Martin, W. C., V. L. Bengtson, and A. A. Acock
1973 "Alienation and age: A context-specific approach." Social Forces (in press).

McCall, G. and J. L. Simmons
1966 Identities and Interaction. New York: Free Press.

McTavish, D. G.
1971 "Perceptions of old people: a review of research methodologies and findings." Gerontologist 11, 4 (Part 2):90-102.

Mead, G. H.
1934 Mind, Self and Society. Chicago: Univ. of Chicago Press.

Neugarten, B. L.
1965a "Personality and patterns of aging." Gawein 13:249-256. (Reprinted in Neugarten, 1968, pp. 173-177).
1965b "Personality changes in the aged." Catholic Psychological Record 3:9-17.
1968 "Adult personality: toward a psychology of the life cycle." In Middle Age and Aging, ed. B. L. Neugarten. Chicago: Univ. of Chicago Press.
1969 "Continuities and discontinuities of psychological issues into adult life." Human Development 12, 2:121-130.

Neugarten, B. L., W. J. Crotty, and S. S. Tobin
1964 "Personality types in an aged population." In Personality in Middle and Later Life, ed. B. L. Neugarten. New York: Atherton.

Neugarten, B. L. and N. D. Datan
1973 "Sociological perspectives on the life cycle." In Life-Span Developmental Psychology: Personality and Socialization, ed. P. Baltes and W. Schaie. New York: Academic Press (forthcoming).

Neugarten, B. L., R. J. Havighurst, and S. S. Tobin
1961 "The measurement of life satisfaction." Journal of Gerontology 16:134-143.

Neugarten, B. L. and J. Moore
1968 "The changing age status system." In Middle Age and Aging, ed. B. L. Neugarten. Chicago: Univ. of Chicago Press.

Neugarten, B. L., J. Moore, and J. Lowe
1965 "Age norms, age constraints, and adult socialization." American Journal of Sociology 70:710-717.

Neugarten, B. L. and W. Peterson
1957 "A study of the American age-grade system." Vol 111 in Fourth Congress of the International Association of Gerontology. Firenze, Italy: Tito Mattioli.

Palmore, E.
1968 "The effects of aging on activities and attitudes." Gerontologist 8:259-263.
1971 "Attitudes toward aging as shown by humor." Gerontologist 11, 3:181-186.

Palmore, E. and F. Whittington
1971 "Trends in the relative status of the aged." Social Forces 50, 1:84-91.

Parsons, T.
1942 "Age and sex in the social structure of the United States." American Sociological Review 7:606-616.

Reichard, S., R. Livson, and P. G. Petersen
1962 Aging and Personality. New York: John Wiley.

Riegel, K. F.
1969 "History as a nomothetic science: Some generalizations from theories and research in developmental psychology." Journal of Social Issues 25, 4:99-127.

Riley, M. W., A. Foner, and associates
1968 Aging and Society, Vol. 1: An Inventory of Research Findings. New York: Russell Sage Foundation.

Riley, M. W., M. Johnson, and A. Foner
1972 Aging and Society, Vol. 3: A Sociology of Age Stratification. New York: Russell Sage Foundation.

Rose, A. M.
1964 "A current theoretical issue in social gerontology." Gerontologist 4:25-29.
1965 "The subculture of the aging." In Older People and Their Social World, ed. A. M. Rose and W. A. Peterson. Philadelphia: F. A. Davis.

Rosow, I.
1967 Social Integration of the Aged. New York: The Free Press.
1973 Socialization to Old Age. Berkeley: Univ. of California Press.

Secord, P. and C. W. Backman
1961 "Personality theory and the problem of stability and change in individual behavior: An interpersonal approach." Psychological Review 68:21-32.

Seltzer, M. M. and R. C. Atchley
1971 "The concept of old: changing attitudes and stereotypes." Gerontologist 11, 3:226-230.

Spence, D. L. and T. D. Lonner
1971 "The empty nest: a transition to motherhood." Family Coordinator 20:369-375.

Strauss, A. L.
1969 Mirrors and Masks: The Search for Identity. San Francisco: Sociology Press.

Streib, G. F.
1965 "Are the aged a minority group?" In Applied Sociology, ed. A. W. Gouldner and S. M. Miller. New York: Macmillan.

Streib, G. F. and C. J. Schneider, Jr.
1971 Retirement in American Society. Ithaca, N. Y.: Cornell Univ. Press.

Tibbitts, C., ed.
1960 Handbook of Social Gerontology. Chicago: Univ. of Chicago Press.

Tobin, S. S. and B. L. Neugarten
1961 "Life satisfaction and social interaction in the aging." Journal of Gerontology 16, 4:344-346.

Trela, J. E.
1971 "Some political consequences of senior center and other old age group memberships." Gerontologist 11, 2:118-124.

Williams, R. and C. Wirths
1965 Lives Through the Years. New York: Atherton.

Wood, V.
1971 "Age-appropriate behavior for older people." Gerontologist 11, 4:74-78.

Zusman, J.
1966 "Some explanations of the changing appearance of psychotic patients: antecedents of the social breakdown syndrome concept." The Millbank Memorial Fund Quarterly 64, 1, 2 (January).

Suggested Readings

Atchley, R. A. 1972 The Social Forces in Later Life: An Introduction to Social Gerontology. Belmont, Calif.: Wadsworth. This is a comprehensive, well-written, and up-to-date introduction to the study of later life. Consideration is given to psychological and biological aging, although the bulk of the book covers age changes in specific situational contexts and the response of social institutions to such changes. Excellent for undergraduate courses, for practitioners seeking a comprehensive introduction, and for graduate students.

Birren, J. E. 1964 The Psychology of Aging. New York: Prentice-Hall. This is the most comprehensive introduction to research on psychological aspects of aging. The author reviews a variety of age changes in psychological functions and capacities, presenting a solid foundation for experimental research in aging. Useful for graduate and upper-division undergraduate courses.

Neugarten, B. L. 1968 Middle Age and Aging: A Reader in Social Psychology. Chicago: Univ. of Chicago Press. This collection brings together 62 research articles on a wide variety of topics regarding social-psychological issues in aging. The editor's comments introducing each section are particularly useful. This is a valuable sourcebook for research and an excellent textbook (available in paperback).

Riley, M. W., A. Foner, and associates. 1968 Aging and Society, Vol. 1: An Inventory of Research Findings. New York: The Russell Sage Foundation. This is a well-organized encyclopedia of social research regarding middle-aged and older people. Hundreds of studies are reviewed in a well-organized framework that summarizes issues as well as findings. Organized into four main parts that deal with (1) the societal context, (2) the aging organism, (3) the personality of the individual, (4) the social roles linking the individual to society. An invaluable sourcebook for anyone doing research (or term papers) in the field of aging.

Riley, M. W., M. Johnson, and A. Foner. 1972 Aging and Society, Vol. 3: A Sociology of Age Stratification. New York: Russell Sage Foundation. This is an exciting book for sociologists interested in aging, for it presents a comprehensive model that attempts to interrelate much of the social phenomena of aging using traditional sociological concepts. The first sections are rough going for anyone without some considerable background in sociology, but the middle chapters—on policy, the work force, the community, higher education, and friendship—are useful for students at any level. This book will influence research in the sociology of aging for years to come as the model it presents is revised and expanded.

THE BOBBS-MERRILL REPRINT SERIES

The author recommends for supplementary reading the following related material. Please fill out this form and mail.

Indicate number of reprints desired

____ **Becker, Howard S.** 1953 "Becoming a Marihuana User." American Journal of Sociology, pp. 235-242. **S-9**/66418 40¢

____ **Becker, Howard S.** 1958 "Problems of Inference and Proof in Participant Observation." American Sociological Review, pp. 652-660. **S-337**/66715 40¢

____ **Becker, Howard, S. and Anselm L. Strauss** 1967 "Careers, Personality, and Adult Socialization," American Journal of Sociology, pp. 253-263. **S-11**/66420 40¢

____ **Benedict, Ruth** 1938 "Continuities and Discontinuities in Cultural Conditioning," Psychiatry, pp. 161-167. **S-18**/66427 40¢

____ **Bott, Elizabeth** 1955 "Urban Families: Conjugal Roles and Social Networks," Human Relations, pp. 345-384. **S-554**/66931 60¢

____ **Chaddock, Robert E.** 1936 "Age and Sex in Population Analysis," The Annals, pp. 185-193. **S-356**/66734 40¢

____ **Coleman, James S.** 1960 "The Adolescent Subculture and Academic Achievement," American Journal of Sociology, pp. 337-347. **S-361**/66739 40¢

____ **Davis, Kingsley** 1940 "The Sociology of Parent-Youth Conflict," American Sociological Review, pp. 523-535. **S-67**/66473 40¢

____ **Elkin, Frederick and William A. Westley** 1955 "The Myth of Adolescent Culture," American Sociological Review, pp. 680-684. **S-79**/66484 40¢

____ **Empey, LaMar T. and Jerome Rabow** 1961 "The Provo Experiment in Delinquency Rehabilitation," American Sociological Review, pp. 679-695. **S-385**/66763 40¢

____ **Glick, Paul C.** 1947 "The Family Cycle," American Sociological Review, pp. 164-174. **S-96**/66501 40¢

____ **Kuhn, Manford H.** 1960 "Self-Attitudes by Age, Sex, and Professional Training," Sociological Quarterly, pp. 39-55. **S-156**/66557 40¢

_____ **Linton, Ralph** 1942 "Age and Sex Categories," American Sociological Review, pp. 589-603.   **S-173**/66572   40¢

_____ **Parsons, Talcott** 1942 "Age and Sex in the Social Structure of the United States," American Sociological Review, pp. 604-616.   **S-217**/66613   40¢

_____ **Ryder, Norman B.** 1965 "The Cohort as a Concept in the Study of Social Change." American Sociological Review, pp. 843-861.   **S-621**/66998   40¢

_____ **Thompson, Wayne and Gordon Streib** 1961 "Meaningful Activity in a Family Context," In Aging and Leisure: A Research Perspective into the Meaningful Use of Time, ed. R. W. Kleemeier. New York: Oxford University Press, pp. 177-211.   **S-521**/66898   60¢

_____ **Wrong, Dennis H.** 1961 "The Oversocialized Conception of Man in Modern Sociology." American Sociological Review, pp. 183-193.   **S-653**/67030   40¢

The Bobbs-Merrill Company, Inc.
College Division
4300 West 62nd Street
Indianapolis, Indiana 46268

Instructors ordering for class use will receive _upon request_ a complimentary desk copy of each title ordered in quantities of 10 or more. Refer to author and _complete_ letter-number code when ordering reprints.

☐ Payment enclosed   ☐ Bill me (on orders for $5 or more only)

_____ Course number   _____ Expected enrollment

☐ For examination   ☐ Desk copy

Bill To_____

ADDRESS_____

CITY_____ STATE_____ ZIP_____

Ship To_____

ADDRESS_____

CITY_____ STATE_____ ZIP_____

Please send me _____ copies of the sociology reprints catalog.

Please send me related reprints catalogs in_____

Any reseller is free to charge whatever price he wishes for our books.

For your convenience please use complete form when placing your order.